FOOTBALL

Chris Brazier

NEW INTERNATIONALIST

Trigger Issues: Football
First published in the UK in 2007 by
New Internationalist™ Publications Ltd
55 Rectory Road,
Oxford OX4 1BW, UK
www.newint.org
New Internationalist is a registered trade mark.

Series editor: Troth Wells
Design by New Internationalist Publications Ltd.

 Printed on recycled paper by T J International, Cornwall, UK
who hold environmental accreditation ISO 14001.

Cover image: Kimimasa Mayama / Reuters

British Library Cataloguing-in-Publication Data.
A catalogue record for this book is available from the British Library.

Library of Congress Cataloguing-in-Publication Data.
A catalogue for this book is available from the Library of Congress.

ISBN: 978-1-904456-77-3

FOOTBALL

Chris Brazier is a co-editor of **New Internationalist** magazine. He also writes regularly for UNICEF and is the author of the *No-Nonsense Guide to World History*.

Trigger Issues
One small item – one giant impact

Other titles:
Condom
Diamonds
Kalashnikov
Mosquito
T-shirt

About the New Internationalist
The **New Internationalist** is an independent not-for-profit publishing co-operative. Our mission is to report on issues of global justice. We publish informative current affairs and popular reference titles, complemented by world food, photography and gift books as well as calendars, diaries, maps and posters – all with a global justice world view.

If you like this **Trigger Issue** book you'll also love the **New Internationalist** magazine. Each month it takes a different subject such as Trade Justice, Nuclear Power or Iraq, exploring and explaining the issues in a concise way; the magazine is full of photos, charts and graphs as well as music, film and book reviews, country profiles, interviews and news.

To find out more about the **New Internationalist**, visit our website at:
www.newint.org

Contents

Introduction

In November 2005 I revisited Garango, a small provincial town in the southeast of Burkina Faso, in West Africa. I was on a special mission for *New Internationalist* magazine, returning to a nearby village that I had come to know well in the summer of 1985 and to which I had already made one return, in 1995. In the mid-1980s Garango and its surrounding villages had seemed about as far removed as could possibly be imagined from the rich world. Water had to be drawn up from wells and then transported huge distances by women carrying vast metal bowls; people scraped at the baked earth without even animals to help them turn it over; clinics and schools were rudimentary, if they existed at all. By 2005 there had been many changes, most of them for the better – functioning schools and clinics, many more water pumps, even mobile phones.

Most of the surprises were pleasant ones. Yet there was one rude shock: I encountered Arsenal shirts on the streets of Garango. If there were one place on earth, I muttered under my breath, where I might have expected to be free from this sight it was here. There weren't only Arsenal shirts, of course: most teenage boys on the streets of Garango wore replica football shirts in the colors of Europe's premier teams. Ragged, ersatz versions, of course, but there they were, with the names of distant legends like Ronaldinho, del Piero and Beckham on their backs. And on the flickering TV in the local bar – electricity had finally reached the town, though not the surrounding villages, three years before – highlights of football from Europe were shown on a Monday evening.

There are two ways of looking at this – globalization gone mad or interconnected global community – and probably both of them are true in their way. But at the very least it was an object lesson in the almost limitless capacity of football to transcend geography, culture and class.

In my own life it has always transcended most things. My ability as a footballer was modest, to put it charitably, and it was pretty much downhill from the time I scored in a victorious schools cup final at the age of 10. But I grew up in a family with four sons and no daughters, with a father who continued to keep goal into his fifties, and who introduced me to professional football in the time-honored way, by raising the seven-year-old me on to his shoulders at the back of the masses standing on the terraces of our local club, Tottenham Hotspur (Arsenal's north London arch-rivals, for those who didn't understand the earlier reference). At 11, I was fortunate enough to be one of the 100,000 actually there at Wembley in 1966 to see England lift the World Cup for the only time in its history. A fairly traditional male upbringing meant that we were a family not particularly strong on communication, certainly not about our inner lives, and in a very real sense football was the lingua franca of our household.

It has never been so uncomplicated for me since. In the late 1970s, when hooliganism was at its height and I was learning via my relationship and my reading about the implications of feminism and anti-sexism, football began to seem like a negative force in my life, one that I should do my best to 'outgrow'. If it actually was about growing up, then I guess it never happened, and it remains a source of tension in my relationship to this day, despite – and partly because of – my having passed on the torch to my own children. And I can't deny that passionate support of one football club has, over the years, involved at least as much pain and frustration as it has joy.

Up to now this interest has not touched my professional life at all – barring an earnest piece about terrace culture in the 1970s for the music weekly *Melody Maker*, which is where I cut my journalistic teeth. So it's been rather intriguing to turn the eye of internationalism and social-justice campaigning on a world that I normally escape into rather as if it were a parallel universe.

This book owes a great debt to David Goldblatt's *The Ball Is Round: A Global History of Football* (Viking 2006) – a 900-page tour de force which I can thoroughly recommend to anyone whose appetite is whetted by some of the morsels in this much slimmer volume. Other absorbing books about football's place in the world that have helped me are Franklin Foer's *How Football Explains the World* (Arrow 2005) and Eduardo Galeano's *Football in Sun and Shadow* (Fourth Estate 1997/2003).

Football in the 21st century is a very different beast from the one that I first encountered in the 1960s – better in many ways but very much worse in others. But it remains a source of endless fascination – and it is a fascination that much of the world now seems to share.

Chris Brazier
Oxford, 2007

1 Gods, child labor and high art

'All I know of morality I learned
from football.'

ALBERT CAMUS

A football. With apologies to North Americans, the world means by this something round – a hollow sphere inflated by air. It is an iconic product, unquestionably a trigger issue of our times. The game that it makes possible is played on an informal basis in almost every park or patch of wasteground on the planet. If the world has a favorite game, then association football has no real competitor for the honor.

Its professional incarnation incites more passion in more places than any other of the world's sports. The circus around its superstar players – with their bling lifestyle, their palace parties and their celebrity 'wags' (wives and girlfriends) – becomes more extreme and more bizarre with every passing year. The topmost layers of the game ooze money – they draw corporate sponsors and billionaire investors like moths to a flame – and yet all but a few clubs are ludicrously unprofitable. Football has been the plaything of dictators as well as the solace of the poor; it has played a part in wars and in struggles for liberation.

It also pulls in the TV viewers. The World Cup Final, staged every four years, is the closest thing the world has to a collective moment. A staggering three billion viewers were said to have tuned in to the last World Cup Final, in Germany in June 2006.

There is an inevitable hyperbole built into this figure – how many people within households counted as being 'tuned in' were actually pursuing other useful hobbies, taking a nap or doing the washing-up? All the same, it is an impressive statistic. There is nothing comparable in terms of simultaneous global experience in a world in which television viewing is ever more atomized, reduced by multiplicitous channels into ever smaller strands of minority interest. The Olympics also boasts massive viewing figures, but fragmented across myriad different events. The first moon landing would surely have provided such a moment had it happened in 2007, but in 1969 TV was still the province of a privileged few. The 9/11 attacks on New York provided a comparable global moment in which the majority of the world's population can reasonably be assumed to have seen and been seared by the same images – but most people saw them in bits and pieces, in news clips retailed over days and weeks rather than as they happened.

So what on earth is it about football that has so effectively commandeered the world's attention? Why does the endlessly repetitive sight of 22 men chasing a ball around a pitch capture the imagination of so many people from so many different cultural backgrounds?

Among team games, you can't help but think that football's success comes down first and foremost to its utter simplicity. Cricket, baseball and American football all require paraphernalia – bats, big gloves, helmets, and so on. Moreover, they have complex rules that can bamboozle the casual observer. Their very arcaneness has an appeal of its own, so that in learning its language and its idiosyncrasies you become part of a club, a special culture.

Football, in contrast, can be played and understood anywhere, without any equipment other than a round ball. Throw down a couple of sweaters at either end of any piece of wasteground and you have all you need for a satisfying game. Two teams pass the ball to each other and try to kick it between the posts or sweaters at the other end.

Except, you might reasonably point out, that there is something unnatural and less than simple about a game in which only the goalkeeper is allowed to use their hands to control the ball. In basketball, which in some ways has a comparable simplicity and flow, you cannot use your feet or your head. In rugby you can use both hands and feet – but you can only pass the ball backwards. Moreover the ball itself, as in American/Canadian football and Australian rules, is not round but rather is designed to bounce in unpredictable ways.

The 'hand' and 'foot' games came from the same root, as we'll see in the next chapter. But perhaps it was something as simple as football's adoption of a round, soft ball which gave it a head start in the global domination stakes.

The earliest balls

Team ball games have been played for at least three millennia. Who played them first is unclear, though the Aboriginal Australians in what is now Victoria may well have played their kicking game of *marn gook* for thousands of years before they were witnessed by white settlers.

But it was in Central America that ball games arguably achieved their greatest cultural prominence before the modern era. All the great civilizations in the region, from the Olmecs to the Aztecs, attached great importance to a ball game played on a rectangular court in which two teams tried to keep the ball in the air before returning it over a central line to their opponents – a distant relation to modern volleyball. The game itself varied through the ages – in Teotihuacán (100-750) it was played with sticks or bats rather than just parts of the body; the Aztecs (14th-16th century) added decorated stone rings at the side of the court through which the teams had to try to send the ball, akin to modern basketball or netball. For the Maya (800-1400), the game was so sacred that it played a fundamental part in their creation myths (see box next page).

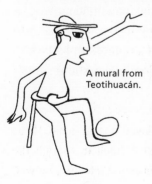

A mural from Teotihuacán.

One reason why ball games had such magical, even sacred, properties for the Mesoamericans was the composition of the ball itself – made of rubber. At

BALL-PLAYING MAYA GODS

According to Mayan text the *Popol Vuh*, two ball-playing mortal brothers were tricked into contesting a ball game against the immortals in the Underworld. They lost and were sacrificed, with the head of one displayed on a tree. The head managed somehow to impregnate a passing goddess, who was duly banished to the mortal world where she gave birth to twins. The twins became wonderful ball-players and eventually had to repeat their father's experience in a big game in the Underworld. They won, and brought back the corpses of their father and uncle, placing them in the sky to become the sun and moon. ◆

that time rubber was only found in the New World, and some unknown genius around 1500 BCE hit upon the idea of mixing latex juices with the roots of the morning glory flower and arrived at a solid, bouncy ball. Columbus brought back rubber balls to show the astonished Spanish court and when Cortés returned from his Aztec conquests in 1528 he brought back ball-players and equipment to entertain King Charles V – an experience sufficient for the Spanish to ajudge the game to be the work of the devil and to suppress it.

Ballplayers in the Old World had to make do with less promising materials. The Chinese of the Han dynasty

A 15th-century Ming dynasty engraving.

(206 BCE onwards) played *cuju* ('kickball'), using a ball made of leather and stuffed with feathers. It involved two teams trying to reach goals at either end of the pitch and involved handling and rough physical contact so may have been more akin to modern rugby than to football. Over the centuries, in the T'ang and Sung dynasties (618-1279), the game became more stylized, with a lighter, hollower ball that had to be kept in the air, but *cuju* seems to have disappeared by the 14th century.

The Romans saved their enthusiasm for gladiatorial combat and chariot races – though their soldiers do seem to have played a rugby-like game called *harpastum*. This or something like it survived into a medieval incarnation, played in Florence. It died out or was banned in the 18th century and thus cannot claim to be a direct ancestor of the modern game – though its heritage provided the name by which football is still known in Italy, *calcio*.

Modern football derives not from any of the great ancient civilizations but rather from the marginalized

Celtic peoples on the fringes of western Europe (though admittedly some speculate that they may have learned it from Roman soldiers playing harpastum). The Celts seem to have played a rough communal game that, far from being confined to a small court like that of the Mesoamericans, involved chasing a ball – usually the sealed and inflated bladder of a pig – across the fields between two villages. These games had local variants in Ireland, Scotland, Wales, Cornwall and Brittany but had certainly infected their Anglo-Saxon and Norman conquerors in England by early medieval times. A 14th-century writer described the game with distaste: 'Young men, in country sport, propel a huge ball not by throwing it into the air but by striking and rolling it along the ground, and that not with their hands but with their feet. A game I say abominable enough, and in my judgment at least, more common, undignified and worthless than any other kind of game, rarely ending but with some loss, accident or disadvantage to the players themselves.'

As this suggests, football was a rough game of the lower classes and was generally frowned upon by the authorities – Edward II, Henry V, Edward IV, Henry VII and Henry VIII all tried to ban it, as did the towns of Halifax, Leicester, Manchester and Liverpool. Generally such attempts to outlaw the game – in Edward IV's case because people should be practising archery in the interests of national defense – failed miserably.

How the ball evolved

We'll come to how this rough rural sport developed into modern football in later chapters but for now let's stick with the ball itself. Pig's bladders provided quite a light and resilient ball but one that could never be perfectly round in shape and was bound to bounce unpredictably. A more reliably round shape could be arrived at by covering the bladder with leather, something that was certainly already happening by Shakespeare's time (see box).

SHAKESPEARE ON FOOTBALL

In *The Comedy of Errors*, written in 1590, the servant Dromio of Ephesus laments the fact that he is beaten by his master in the following terms:

Am I so round with you as you with me
That like a football you spurn me thus?
You spurn me hence, and he will spurn me hither
If I last in this service you must case me in leather.

In *King Lear*, meanwhile, Kent retorts: '*Nor tripped neither,*
you base football player!' ◆

A 450-year-old football from Scotland.

More reliably round balls did not arrive, however, until the industrial vulcanization of rubber, which was patented by US citizen Charles Goodyear in 1844. Goodyear himself designed a rubber ball in 1855 but the first inflatable rubber bladder designed to be contained in a stitched-leather exterior was designed by HJ Lindon – according to probably spurious legend, Lindon's incentive was that his wife had died from lung disease as a result of blowing up hundreds of pigs' bladders.

The rules of the recently formed English Football Association decreed in 1872 that the ball must be 'spherical with a circumference of 27 to 28 inches' (68.6 cm to 71.1 cm), and this remains the official size today, though the required weight of the ball was increased from 13-15 ounces to 14-16 ounces (397-454 gm) in 1937.

Mass production of footballs did not begin until the founding of the English Football League in 1888, when the two main producers were Mitre in Huddersfield (still one of main ball-making companies) and Thomlinson's in Glasgow. The top-grade ball covers were made with leather from a cow's rump while lesser balls were made from the cow's shoulder. These early balls generally comprised two leather sections stitched together at the top and bottom of the ball but the development of multiple interlocking leather panels improved roundness and reliability. Most balls had a tanned leather cover with 18 sections stitched together, arranged in six panels of three strips each.

Ball technology changed relatively little until the second half of the 20th century. A cloth carcass was introduced between the bladder and the leather exterior, again improving the shape, but the bladder still had to be inserted into a 15-centimeter slot which was tied together with laces rather like a boot. In wet weather, water would seep into the leather, making the ball much heavier by the end of the game than it had been at the beginning. These heavy balls often had the consistency of cannonballs and, as late as the 1960s, heading them from a goalkeeper's long kick felt like a punch from a heavyweight boxer – and if you connected with the laces of the ball the experience was even more unpleasant.

Balls could be unreliable – the ball burst fairly regularly, as it did in the English FA Cup finals of both 1946 and 1947, apparently due to the inferior quality of leather in the immediate aftermath of World War Two. And there could be significant local variation: in the first World Cup

Final of 1930, Argentina and Uruguay could not agree on the ball to be used and arranged to change at half-time. Argentina won the first half 2-1 but the Uruguayans scored three times with their own ball in the second half to take the trophy.

The advent of synthetic materials changed the manufacture of footballs completely. First came the introduction of non-porous paint that could coat the leather and help resist water. The first totally synthetic ball debuted in the 1960s, though manufacturers continued to consider that leather was necessary until the late 1980s. Since then, however, synthetic footballs have become virtually universal, with synthetics now emulating the cell structure of leather. Vegetarians (like me) no longer need to feel guilty about kicking a ball around...

Child labor and footballs

There is, however, still something to worry about on the moral/ethical front – the part that child labor continues to play in providing the world's footballs. The synthetic surface of a football is as dependent on the high quality of its hand-stitching as were the earliest balls made in Huddersfield and Glasgow – perhaps even more so given that there are now 26 or 32 panels to be stitched together rather than the former 18. A modern ball has more than 1,800 stitches – and these are done by hand to guarantee even tension in the seams right across the ball.

Given this, it is hardly surprising that, while the main sports companies continue to be based in the industrialized world (Mitre and Umbro from Britain, Adidas and Puma from Germany, Reebok and Nike from the US), the balls made for them come almost exclusively from the Majority World, where the labor is cheaper.

In fact it is estimated that 80 per cent of footballs are made in Pakistan and that three-quarters of these – a staggering two-thirds of all the footballs in the world – are made in one city, Sialkot. The stitching of soccer balls started in Sialkot in the first half of the 20th century, supplying the armed forces of the British Raj, but continued to grow after independence, especially after the 'Tango' ball for the 1982 World Cup was produced there.

The involvement of child labor in ball-stitching became a major issue when activists put the issue on the international agenda in the run-up to the 1996 European Championship. At the time, the hand-sewing of footballs was taking place mainly at home – the 1,800 intricate stitches in each ball would earn workers the princely sum of 27 rupees (then around 50 cents). There was next

THE STITCHER, SIALKOT, PAKISTAN

Johnson is 13 years old. He has two younger brothers and two younger sisters. His father and his uncle work in a brickyard. The meager wages this brings in are insufficient to feed seven people. Johnson has never been to school. His mother started stitching footballs at home, and Johnson started helping her very early.

Since his mother had to take care of the children and the housework, they could only stitch three balls a day, which brought in 45 rupees. The daily needs of the family amount to around 100 rupees. The family started borrowing from neighbors without ever being able to pay back. The hard work at the brickyard eventually ruined the health of the father, who is no longer able to carry out such hard work.

When an informal education center sponsored as part of the Atlanta Agreement opened in Johnson's village, the teacher approached the family. They were quite reluctant to let Johnson stop working, but when they were told that the children only went to school for three hours a day, and that they could go to work for the rest of the day, the family agreed. Johnson has been worried lately because his father is ill again. He doesn't know if he'll be able to continue going to school but he is doing his best. ◆

Samuel Poos, Clean Clothes Campaign,
www.cleanclothes.org

to no supervision of the outsourced labor and children would often participate in the stitching rather than go to school, either with their parents or in workshops. In 1997, a Save the Children survey showed that 81 per cent of the estimated 5,000-7,000 children who stitched footballs did so to meet basic needs such as food, clothing, shelter and education.

Activist pressure and awareness-raising forced the industry to attempt to put its house in order and shore up public confidence. The Atlanta Agreement was concluded between the International Labour Organization, UNICEF and the Sialkot Chamber of Commerce and Industry in 1997, aiming to ensure that no child labor was used in the production of footballs. The minimum amount paid per ball was increased to 47 rupees and UNICEF and local NGOs were delegated to help children into school and compensate families for the loss of their children's labor. In addition, production was supposed to be centralized rather than delegated to homeworkers so that it could be monitored.

By the end of 1999, 58 sportswear firms had committed themselves to buying footballs only from companies accepting ILO monitoring, while 53 exporters had joined the prevention program. More than 600 monitored stitching centers had been opened, including 150 for women.

So far so good, you might think – an exemplary case of transnational corporations being forced by activist pressure into improving their standards and the conditions of their workers. And to a point this is true.

Yet in November 2006 Nike was forced to announce that it was sacking its main manufacturer of hand-stitched balls, the Pakistani company Saga Sports, due to 'significant labor compliance violations'. This was a roundabout way of saying that Saga was still outsourcing production to homeworkers – and that many of the balls used in the English Premiership, Nike's most prestigious footballing contract, were probably stitched by children.

In practice it is evident that some child labor has been pushed into more remote villages of the region, beyond the reach of inspectors – as well as migrating into the surgical instruments industry there, which was not covered by the Atlanta Agreement. The main causes of child labor in Pakistan – such as family poverty and local workers' inability to organize – remain untouched.

The immediate way forward for Nike was to shift production from Pakistan to China, where the corporation will certainly not be troubled by pesky independent trade unions.

The long-term way forward may have been signaled by the 2006 World Cup in Germany, for which Adidas provided new match balls that had been 'thermally bonded' and machine pressed instead of traditionally stitched. This hi-tech solution is unlikely to be offered by Pakistani producers any time soon. Doubtless this development will salve the consciences of individual consumers and make things easier for corporate PR officers, but whether it will improve the lives of poor families in the Sialkot area is altogether more questionable.

The world's ball game

In its way football has become as central to the global culture of the 21st century as it was to the local Mayan culture of the 11th century. The game has, of course, its own history, its own leaders, its own burning issues, and these can loom larger in many people's lives than those of the mainstream world – for many people the back pages of a newspaper are read before the front, if the front pages are read at all. But the crossover between those two worlds has become bigger with every passing decade. Modern politicians and dictators tend not to ban the game like the kings of old – Maoist China and Khomeini's Iran aside – but rather to co-opt it and harness its popular power to their own ends. Today's billionaires increasingly see it as a testing ground for their egos, a new popular arena for their power. Footballers are more famous and more pampered even than movie stars – and have access at a

---

FOOTBALL AS ART: BRAZIL IN 1970

At its most dreary, on a rainy winter's night in Katowice or Hartlepool, football can be insufferably basic, reduced to its bare essentials of physical endeavor, the ball continually hoofed up in the air in search of a head, all sound and fury signifying absolutely nothing, not even a single goal.

But set against that must be its moments of sublime skill that cause a sharp intake of breath in bodies all over the world, that thanks to the wonders of instant visual transmission live in the minds of millions effectively as works of art. There are innumerable examples of individual brilliance that could qualify but the apogee of football as high art was a team performance and, ultimately, a team goal. It came in Mexico City in June 1970 when Brazil won the World Cup Final 4-1 against an Italian team as noted for their defensive cynicism as their opponents were celebrated for representing romance, spontaneity and the 'beautiful game'.

Two philosophies of life hold each other in check for three-

---

younger age to the most improbable wealth. The violence and ethnic hatred within the game itself have mirrored such problems in wider society.

These are all negatives. Where are the positives? Let us leave it for the moment at one: football as art.

quarters of the game, but Brazil suddenly cut loose, scoring twice in five minutes, and ultimately celebrate their victory with an unspeakably glorious final goal. Clodoaldo beats four players in a mazy dribble in his own half – divine inspiration descending upon a mere mortal – before feeding it forward; Jairzinho jinks inside, beats one and evades another as he passes to Pele (pictured); the iconic inside left pauses thoughtfully and then rolls a perfectly weighted pass into the path of his captain, Carlos Alberto, who surges unstoppably forward to hit the ball clean, clear and true in the corner with all the force of history. No words can do it justice, but the golden shirts against the green grass on that June day, encapsulated in video compilations of great goals or in grainy miniature on YouTube, are a match for the studio work of any Grand Master. ◆

2 Empire and goal rush

> 'I have never seen such enthusiasm for the game as shown by the two republics and everywhere one sees the hold it has taken on the people. Boys on the street, on the seashore, down alleys, soldiers on barrack grounds – all have the fever.'
>
> THE MANAGER OF SWINDON TOWN, TOURING ARGENTINA AND URUGUAY IN 1912.

So how did the village-to-village kick, rush and push of the Celts and Anglo-Saxons become the world's favorite game? And why did a few notable areas of the globe resist its blandishments?

At the outset of the 19th century, with industrialization and urbanization just beginning to gather pace, there seemed little likelihood that football would emerge as the leading sport in England, let alone the rest of the world. An authoritative survey of English sports and pastimes

76239

written in 1801 barely noticed it in passing, saying: 'The game was formerly much in vogue among the common people, though of late years it seems to have fallen into disrepute and is but little practised.'

The disrepute was clear. Puritanical religious movements were concerned to rein in the anarchic pleasures of the working classes. And as people continued to be drawn from the countryside into urban areas, increasingly powerful city authorities all over the country opposed football on the grounds that it was dangerous and involved the participation of a 'lawless rabble'. In 1835 street football in urban areas was banned by law, though it seems to have survived in isolated pockets, most notably in the city of Sheffield.

Ironically, given that it had hitherto been a game of the common people, football's survival and transformation into the codified sport of today was due to the most privileged institutions in Britain – the private schools. Despite housing and educating the boys who were to provide the next generation of the ruling class, these were fairly brutal places. Both the discipline and the boys' own culture was extremely violent, and rough games involving balls had been imported into most of these schools by the beginning of the 19th century, where they developed

their own informal rules and traditions.

As the Victorian era took hold, forward-thinking teachers began to see a central role for team sports in developing a new kind of young man, suitable for conquering and administering the British Empire – not to mention diverting their adolescent energies away from masturbation and homosexuality. By the mid-19th century team sports had become arguably more important than any kind of classroom learning to major private schools such as Eton, Rugby and Charterhouse.

But each school had its own rules. While Eton and Charterhouse, for example, mainly (though not exclusively) kicked the ball, Rugby and Marlborough mainly handled it. This caused major problems when boys from those schools then came together at university or in the army and led to an early attempt to come up with rules that compromised between all the various forms, at Cambridge in 1846. Bitter debate continued, and all attempts at compromise foundered on the rivalry between the various academic institutions.

It was not until November 1863 that 'old boys' from various private schools arranged a meeting in London at the Freemasons' Tavern in Lincoln's Inn Fields and started the process of arriving at a unified code for the game. Discussions continued over the ensuing months, wrestling not only with the irreconcilable difference between the hand and foot games but also with the question of whether kicking the opponent's shins should be allowed – this practice, known as 'hacking', was considered a vital part of the game by many. Eventually the rules produced by this group, which called itself the Football Association, outlawed hacking as well as carrying the ball – though they did initially allow someone to catch the ball and call

The Royal Engineers team that played in the 1872 FA Cup.

out 'mark' as a way of winning a free kick.

The Football Association's rules were not the first – Sheffield Football Club had come up with its own set in 1858. But when the Sheffield and London FAs thrashed out their differences, and when the still-dissident handling enthusiasts established the separate rules of rugby in 1871, the stage was at last set for an 11-a-side game that could be played across the country according to the same precepts.

The FA Cup

The first FA Challenge Cup (right) in 1872 was contested by 15 teams, most of them from London, though the first Scottish club, Queen's Park from Glasgow, did make it to the semi-finals. The Cup was won by a club comprising old boys from Harrow School, called The Wanderers. It took place at The Oval cricket ground and was attended by 2,000 people, who would have witnessed a rather different game from the one we are used to. The early 'gentleman amateurs' considered the game to be about dribbling the ball and considered passing it to a team-mate to be rather dishonorable. Partly for this reason, it was rare that the ball was hit in the air or headed. Barging into an opponent, including the goalkeeper, to knock them over was considered an integral part of the game.

By now football was spreading like wildfire throughout Britain – and its incendiary popularity meant that the heyday of the upper-class gentleman footballer was a very short one. As one example, Darwen football club emerged when former pupils of Harrow returning to their family estate in Lancashire taught working-class boys in this

HOW THE GAME CHANGED

1872 The early formal games were often played on much bigger pitches – they could be as much as 100 yards (91m) wide and 200 yards (182m) long. The limits of the pitch were marked by flags. The goalposts at the first FA Cup Final had no bar, just tape strung across the top, and that was itself a recent innovation, with goals previously being allowed no matter how high they passed between the posts.

1874 Umpires were introduced, one from each club on the sidelines – there was no referee until 1881, when he simply acted as arbiter between the two club umpires.

1882 A fixed crossbar was introduced and white lines were marked on the pitch, including a halfway line. Goalkeepers could still at this stage handle the ball anywhere in their own half. Throw-ins from the sidelines now had to be two-handed.

1887 The penalty kick was introduced to punish fouls committed within 12 yards of goal – though it could be taken anywhere cotton town how to play. They played the game so well that they took Old Etonians to two replays in the FA Cup quarter-final of 1879. Lancashire was a key hub of the working-class game, which soon produced big clubs such as Blackburn Rovers, Preston North End – and Burnley, which was already drawing crowds of 12,000 by 1884.

The influx of working-class teams quickly changed the

---

along the 12-yard line. A center circle now ensured that the opposition kept their distance at kick-off.

1891 The independent referee was given control of the game and allowed on to the pitch – though he still had to wait for captains to call for a foul before awarding it. A goal net was introduced.

1898 The referee was given full powers and neutral line judges were introduced.

1902 The 12-yard penalty line was replaced by an 18-yard-by-44-yard penalty box.

1909 Goalkeepers were for the first time required to wear a different-colored shirt.

1912 Goalkeepers were restricted to handling the ball in the penalty area.

1937 A 'D' was added to the penalty box to ensure opponents kept their distance while the kick was taken.

1939 Shirt numbers became compulsory. ◆

Blackburn Rovers' FA Cup-winning team from 1886.

style of the game as it became plain that passing to team-mates so as to maneuver the ball around the pitch, make use of the wings and play high balls for players to head towards goal was a much more fluid and effective way of playing. In the 1882 FA Cup Final the Old Etonians, playing the old dribbling game, beat Blackburn Rovers, pioneers of the passing game. It was a last hurrah – in 1883 the Etonians were beaten in the final by Blackburn Olympic, which contained weavers, spinners, a plumber and a publican, and who took the game seriously enough to train on the sands at Blackpool for five days and diet on kippers, porridge, beer and oysters.

The first professionals

Hand in hand with the involvement of working-class players came the advent of professionalism. The FAs in both Sheffield and London were still steeped in the culture of amateurism that derived from the private schools. But with ever-increasing crowds prepared to pay to watch the leading teams, professional football very quickly became an unstoppable force. At first the payments were under the counter or by way of jobs in local firms but the migration of players to play for the richer and more popular clubs in other areas was remarkable – as early as 1883 Preston had ten Scots in their first team and Burnley nine.

In 1884, 31 of the leading clubs, most of them from Lancashire and the West Midlands, threatened to form their own association that would allow professionalism and the following year the FA caved in.

The next step towards global domination was the formation of a league in which clubs would play each other home and away over the course of a season. This is so natural a part of our way of looking at things that it is easy to forget that until as late as the 1980s rugby union was still organized on an 'amateur' basis, with teams playing 'friendlies' against each other – though on the other side of the coin baseball in the US had already set up a professional league by the 1870s. The Football League emerged at the instigation of a Scottish director of Aston Villa, William McGregor, who invited six clubs from Lancashire and six from the Midlands to a meeting in Manchester in April 1888. They agreed to form a league, which duly kicked off on the dot of three o'clock on Saturday 8 September 1888.

THE FIRST LEAGUE

The founder members of the English Football League were:

Accrington
Aston Villa
Blackburn Rovers
Bolton Wanderers
Burnley
Derby County
Everton
Notts County
Preston North End
Stoke City
West Bromwich Albion
Wolverhampton Wanderers

Clubs bearing these names play to this day in the four top divisions of English football, though Accrington Stanley is a different outfit from that of the original founders. ◆

Crowd numbers at football matches ballooned through the early decades, from the 600,000 attending League games in the first season to the five million that turned up to what was by then the First Division in 1905-06. Clubs had to build stadiums to accommodate them, and newspapers and magazines to serve and foster the interests of the football-going public proliferated all over the country. Admission prices went up to sixpence in 1890, which was more expensive than the music hall at the time, though still pitched at a level that would allow most ordinary people to attend. The crowds were overwhelmingly male, though clubs' original decision to allow women to attend for free was rescinded in 1884 when 2,000 women turned up to watch Preston play.

But even this spectacular development paled compared with the rise of the game in Scotland. This was centered on the city of Glasgow, where stadiums had continually to expand to cater for the vast numbers wanting to attend. The early internationals between Scotland and England provide an index of soaring public interest: the first, in 1872, drew a crowd of 3,500; by 1878 a ground capacity of 20,000 was easily filled; by the 1890s Celtic had built a ground big enough to hold 63,000, and by 1907 Hampden Park had been rebuilt to accommodate over 121,000, the

largest stadium in the world.

Imperial spread

Almost as soon as it gained a foothold in Britain, the game began to percolate out into other countries and cultures. The informal vehicle of transmission was the Empire. Britain was at this point seen as the most dynamic, modern country in the world, and it is difficult to appreciate from a 21st-century vantage-point just how cool and progressive anything British – or, usually, English, since the distinction between the two was rarely made – was seen to be. Elites in many parts of the world were influenced by and aimed to emulate the English, and Britain's commercial reach meant that there were usually expatriate communities available to provide a model. Football's original identity as a game of the private-school, empire-administering class helped it enormously to cross the seas.

WORLD RECORD TRANSFERS

(in pounds sterling, thanks to the British origins of the earliest stars)

- First £1,000 player – Alf Common (left), Sunderland to Middlesbrough, 1905
- First £10,000 player – David Jack, Bolton to Arsenal, 1929
- First £100,000 player – Luis Suárez, Barcelona to Inter Milan, 1961
- First £1,000,000 player – Giuseppe Savoldi, Bologna to Napoli, 1975
- First £5,000,000 player – Diego Maradona, Barcelona to Napoli, 1984
- First £10,000,000 player – Jean-Pierre Papin, Marseille to AC Milan, 1992
- First £20,000,000 player – Denílson de Oliveira Araújo, São Paulo to Real Betis, 1998
- First £30,000,000 player – Christian Vieri, Lazio to Inter Milan, 1999
- First £40,000,000 player – Zinedine Zidane (right), Juventus to Real Madrid, 2001 ◆

The earliest acolytes were in Denmark and Holland, both of which had extremely anglophile inclinations in the late 1800s. The Danes created the first European football association in 1889 and the game quickly spread beyond high society to workers' teams, producing players

THE SUPPRESSION OF WOMEN'S FOOTBALL

Football was perceived as 'a man's game' from the start, and the Victorian British considered it an inappropriate pastime for the 'fairer sex' – one that would probably be harmful to their 'delicate constitution'. Nevertheless some upper-class women started playing anyway – there were formal games in Scotland in 1892 and in England in 1895. Any chance of development was nipped in the bud, however, by outright repression. The Dutch

FA banned women's football at its affiliated stadiums in 1896 and the English FA ruled that men's teams could not play against women in 1902.

The influx of women to the industrial workforce during the First World War nevertheless led to an upsurge of women's football,

Dick Kerr's Ladies in action.

good enough to take the Olympic silver medal (behind England) in both 1908 and 1912. A little later the game was enthusiastically adopted in Switzerland, and in Austria, where the Austro-Hungarian Empire meant that it spread fast and naturally to Budapest and Prague.

inspired by the example of Dick Kerr's Ladies, a team based on the workforce in a Preston factory. By 1921 there were at least 150 teams and a Ladies' Football Association was launched in Blackburn. A staggering 53,000 watched Dick Kerr's Ladies beat St Helens Ladies at Everton's ground, Goodison Park, in 1920.

Sadly, the English FA's response to this explosion was to feel threatened by it and to slap it down: women's clubs were banned from playing in men's stadiums in 1921 and excluded from any coaching or financial support.

In this impossible situation, women's football withered on the vine and as late as the 1920s *The Lancet* medical journal was able to get away with the ridiculous assertion that football was dangerous for the female body.

It was to take until the 1990s – ironically, partly in response to the success of women's soccer in the US – for women's football in England to recover some momentum and for big clubs such as Arsenal, Charlton and Fulham to begin taking their women's branches seriously. ◆

But the game also quickly reached South America through the sailors and traders who visited its Atlantic ports. In Brazil a journalist described the phenomenon in the following terms: 'A group of Englishmen, a bunch of maniacs as they all are, get together, from time to time, to kick around something that looks like a bull's bladder. It gives them great satisfaction or fills them with sorrow when this kind of yellowish bladder enters a rectangle formed by wooden posts.' But the penetration was swifter still in Argentina and Uruguay, where British participation in the economic exploitation of the rich mineral and agricultural resources meant that by 1880 there were 40,000 Britons in Buenos Aires alone.

Wherever football spread in the late 19th and early 20th centuries, it followed a similar pattern. Promoted by individual enthusiasts – like the Swiss Hans Kamper who founded FC Barcelona with a group of other Swiss and British players in 1899 – it tended to be adopted by the local élite, which lent it a certain respectability and cachet, before spreading like wildfire to lower classes who immediately relished its fluidity and the ease with which it could be played even on the roughest waste ground. The British connection was almost always vital to establishing the initial bridgehead – as with the two earliest clubs to emerge in Italy, Genoa and AC Milan, which retain to this day the anglicized spelling rather than the local Genova and Milano.

Wherever it took hold, football very quickly became genuinely a people's game. It was helped in this by the cataclysm of the First World War, which marked the end of the old order all over Europe. In its wake, working-class rights began to be asserted and the granting of a shorter working week meant that Saturday became a half-day and made it possible for football to take place in the afternoon – something the British working class had been granted a generation before.

Why did some countries remain immune?
Football is unquestionably the world's game but there remain key outposts where it has struggled to be accepted. If its appeal was so instantaneous that it could proliferate even in the most unpromising terrain given just an enthusiastic individual teacher with a ball brought from across the water, why did it so conspicuously fail at first to make a mark in North America, Australasia, South Africa – and even in its original Celtic heartlands of Ireland and Wales?

The English connotations of the game may have been

CREOLE FOOTBALL

The process was unstoppable. Like the tango, football blossomed in the slums. It required no money and could be played with nothing more than sheer desire. In fields, in alleys and on beaches, native-born kids and young immigrants improvised games using balls made of old socks filled with rags or paper, and a couple of stones for a goal. Thanks to the language of the game, which soon became universal, workers driven out of the countryside could communicate perfectly well with workers driven out of Europe. The Esperanto of the ball connected poor Creoles with *peons* who had crossed the sea from Vigo, Lisbon, Naples, Beirut or Besarabia with their dreams of 'hacer la América' – making a new world by building, carrying, baking or sweeping. Football had made a lovely voyage: first organized in the colleges and universities of England, it brought joy to the lives of South Americans who had never set foot in a school.

On the fields of Buenos Aires and Montevideo, a style was born. A home-grown way of playing football, like the home-grown way of dancing which was being invented in the *milonga* [tango] clubs. Dancers drew filigrees on a single floor tile, and football players created their own language in that tiny space where they chose to retain and possess the ball rather than kick it, as if their feet were hands braiding the leather. On the feet of the first Creole virtuosos *el toque*, the touch, was born: the ball was strummed as if it were a guitar, a source of music.

At the same time, football was being tropicalized in Rio

de Janeiro and São Paulo by the poor who enriched it while they appropriated it. No longer the possession of the few comfortable youths who played by copying, this foreign sport became Brazilian, fertilized by the creative energies of the people discovering it. And thus was born the most beautiful football in the world, made of hip feints, undulations of the torso and legs in flight, all of which came from *capoeira*, the warrior dance of black slaves, and from the joyful dances of the big-city slums. ◆

Eduardo Galeano, from *Football in Sun and Shadow* (Fourth Estate 1997/2003).

An early photo of the *capoeira* dance.

as responsible for this as they were for its acceptance elsewhere. Certainly in Ireland the burgeoning nationalist movement saw the game as a symbol of English oppression and consciously promoted their own games of hurling and Gaelic football as a matter of national pride – though, curiously, rugby did not bear the same stigma, despite being ultimately much more associated with the English ruling class. Only in 2007 was the Irish soccer team finally accorded the honour of playing in Dublin's finest stadium, Croke Park – itself named after the Archbishop who had led the campaign against England's 'vicious' sports and literature.

In Britain's other emigrant colonies – Australia, New Zealand, South Africa and Canada – there was not such hostility towards the 'mother country' as in Ireland but emergent national pride still played a part in football's rejection. Australia had already developed its own variant of football very early on and actually produced a set of rules for it in Melbourne in 1859, four years before the English FA produced their version. Canada was ultimately influenced more by the top US universities and their version of football than that from Britain – though its real enthusiasm was preserved for ice hockey, a more appropriate winter sport given the local climate. New

Zealand/Aotearoa had a relatively small population and possibly there was no room for more than one winter game; the early choice of rugby by schools and colleges was confirmed by the early victories of its national team, the All-Blacks, over the British. The achievements of the South African Springboks had the same effect, though in this case the adoption of rugby rather than football had much to do with class and race consciousness – in a highly stratified society, football's working-class associations and its early appeal to black people in the colony made it anathema to the white ruling class.

In the US the failure of soccer to take hold remains somewhat surprising given its vast urban population and its early industrialization. But baseball was already long established as the national sport by the time the upstart game came on the scene, and the window for a winter game was filled when Harvard encountered rugby in a match with a Canadian university in 1874 and proceeded not only to develop its own variant but to persuade the other élite colleges to adopt the new game of American football. Soccer has continued to be played by ordinary people but numerous attempts to establish a professional league that could showcase the game's virtues fell flat right the way through the 20th century.

FOOTBALL COMICS

Wherever football has been popular, so too have been children's comics dedicated to it. The archetype is the British comic *Roy of the Rovers*, whose changing hair fashions over the decades are illustrated on the covers below. But Italy has plenty of its own equivalents, as does every other football-mad nation – and Ronaldinho now has a Brazilian children's comic dedicated just to him. ◆

Africa's anti-colonial game

Africa has embraced football with fervor – there is no real competitor to it as the continental game. Yet the early Bantu-speaking peoples had no word for ball and ball games seem not to have been played except by the San in the far south and the Ethiopians, Egyptians and Berbers in the north.

As elsewhere, the game arrived with the representatives of the British Empire – first sailors, then colonial armies and police forces, which recruited Africans and taught them the rules of football and boxing, and finally schools. A government school in Gold Coast (now Ghana) produced the first-ever black African football club, which beat a team of British civil servants 3-1 in 1903 and inspired a raft of imitators, including Hearts of Oak in 1911, which is still one of Ghana's top clubs today.

Africa's pioneer footballing country was undoubtedly Egypt, however. Here the local ruling class instantly adopted the game and played it to an extremely high standard, retaining it as their game of choice once the British had departed after the First World War. Egypt provided the first African team to compete in the Olympics, in 1920, and qualified for the World Cup finals in 1934.

Colonial contact may have provided football's *entrée*, but it was nationalist resistance that caused it to spread all over the continent. Football fields were one of the few places where the colonial authorities allowed Africans to gather freely, and inevitably football clubs became recruiting grounds for burgeoning nationalist movements. The association of the two all over the continent became clear – football became the favored game of nationalist movements from South Africa to Nigeria. And maybe the connection was more than serendipitous. Is it fanciful to think that football was the first environment in which Africans could see that they might organize themselves to play against colonial whites on a level playing field and win?

3 Money, money, money

'When I was in the leverage buy-out business
we bought Weetabix and we leveraged it
up to make our return. You could say that
anyone who was eating Weetabix was
paying for our purchase of Weetabix. It was
just business. It is the same for Liverpool;
revenues come in from whatever source and
go out to whatever source and, if there is
money left over, it is profit.'

LIVERPOOL FOOTBALL CLUB'S US OWNER,
TOM HICKS.

As a telling statement of one man's passion for his
club, Tom Hicks' takes some beating. Hicks is a Texan
entrepreneur, who owns the Dallas Stars ice hockey
team and the Texas Rangers baseball franchise, and is
a longtime crony and backer of George W Bush. But at

least the three interests mentioned in the previous sentence had a local Texas connection. Liverpool FC, on the other hand, resides in a different country, playing a game that Hicks does not even claim to love or understand.

Liverpool has an extraordinary footballing tradition, with five European Cups and a record 18 English League titles to its name; its fans' passion is legendary. The club is considered by many to need extra investment both to fund the development of a bigger stadium and the purchase of players that will ensure it competes at the highest level. For that reason the 2007 takeover by Hicks and his partner George Gillet was initially welcomed by supporters. But it has since emerged that the money paid, £178 million ($350 million), was borrowed from a bank and that the annual interest payments on the debt of £21 million would be paid by the club. 'Hopefully the club will have extra cash flow so they can pay us a dividend to do that,' said Hicks.

This made it exactly the same kind of deal pioneered by another US entrepreneur and sports club owner, Malcolm Glazer, when he bought up Manchester United in 2005 and saddled it with even higher levels of debt – producing significant fan protest (see chapter 5).

The sudden predatory interest of foreign sharks is a new twist in the tale of football club ownership. Clubs have traditionally been run as private companies by rich men prepared to invest the funds they earned outside the game in improving the fortunes of the club they had supported since boyhood. Among many classic examples is the case of Jack Walker, a steel baron who invested millions in restoring the fortunes of his beloved Blackburn Rovers, with such (albeit temporary) success that they won the recently formed English Premiership in 1995 – the only club outside of Manchester United, Arsenal and Chelsea to have done so.

The model remains in place at the lower levels of the game, where clubs leak money and eternally battle against debt for their survival. In the top division, however, the goalposts have been moved. In the 1990s many top clubs took advantage of new capital by launching themselves as public companies on the stock exchange, a major step away from local control.

In the 21st century the idea of local benefactors controlling clubs on behalf of fans has come to seem even more outmoded, as foreign billionaires have taken over clubs with which they had no previous point of contact or affiliation, as with the Russian Roman Abramovich at Chelsea, the Icelander Eggert Magnusson at West Ham and the Thai Thaksin Shinawatra at Manchester City.

TV cash feeds the frenzy

The corporate-style takeover has hit England first –

ABRAMOVICH'S BILLIONS

Roman Abramovich altered the landscape of European football when he took control of Chelsea in 2003 – and few people would consider it a change for the better.

One of the notorious Russian oligarchs – entrepreneurs who made billions from the scandalous sell-off of state assets during the negligent rule of President Boris Yeltsin – he was estimated in January 2007 to have a fortune of $20.7 billion.

Abramovich apparently decided to invest in a football club on a whim, having been intrigued by a match between Manchester United and Real Madrid. Chelsea was not his first choice but was in desperate financial straits and thus easy to pick up. He cleared its debts at a stroke and has since funded the purchase of top stars from all over the world, usually at ludicrously inflated prices. His total investment so far is approaching one billion dollars.

The effect was so immediate as to give the lie to the notion that footballing success cannot be easily bought: Chelsea won

---

mainly because it has the world's most marketable league – but the changes in ownership are indicative of the huge changes in football's global culture. Football in the 21st century is a globalized game and, as in the wider process of globalization, power and money increasingly tend to accrue to the key global 'brands'. It has long been the case

the Premiership in both 2005 and 2006, having only won the English title once in their history before.

This is not the first time that a billionaire has taken a football club as his plaything, nor will it be the last. But Abramovich's intervention has been disturbing in part because it has effectively removed Chelsea from the real world. The club routinely runs with a massive operating deficit that in any other club would make spending hundreds of millions of dollars on transfers and players' contracts impossible. The stated long-term goal is for the business to be self-sustaining but there is absolutely no prospect of that happening any time soon.

For decades Chelsea have had glitzy, 'showbiz' associations but Abramovich's billions have turned it overnight into the club that English fans most love to hate. The sooner Abramovich tires of his plaything the better, most would say. He might perhaps then plough more of his ill-gotten gains into Chukotka, the impoverished Siberian province of which he is governor. ◆

in England that Manchester United have been derided as a club that had more fans in the rest of the country than they did in Manchester itself – but there are almost certainly now far more United fans outside England than in the country itself. The rich are getting richer – and the key to the wealth is television.

Up until the 1990s televised football almost everywhere was provided by a single broadcasting outfit, often owned by the state. There was next to no competition and the football clubs meekly took what they were offered. The change in the landscape came with the advent of cable and satellite subscription channels. In the late 1980s the Canal Plus channel in France demonstrated that offering live football was the single best way of persuading the public to pay for television that they had been accustomed to receiving free.

The bidding wars began – and the money football received from television ballooned accordingly. In Germany, for example, the value of annual TV rights rose from 23 million euros in 1990 to 84 million in 1995 and 168 million in 2000 and now stands at 288 million.

Similar growth has been recorded almost everywhere in Europe, though it was harder to make pay-per-view football stick in Italy, where a majority of viewers managed to get hold of pirated smart cards.

As an exercise in dog-eat-dog capitalism, European football takes some beating. The vast majority of money – around 69 per cent as of 2002 – accrues to five leagues: England, France, Italy, Germany and Spain. When the revenue from the UEFA Champions League was included – which inevitably goes to the top clubs in these five leagues – the proportion swallowed up in 2002 by the big five leagues was 80 per cent.

Sink or swim

Within those countries the rich are getting ever richer too. In England the Football League used to distribute television money to all its member clubs, albeit on a sliding scale. In 1992, however, the top division split away to form a 'Premier' League, a decision largely motivated by the prospect of clubs keeping TV money for themselves – smaller clubs all over the country were left to sink or swim, and many have wrestled with the prospects of bankruptcy and liquidation in the succeeding years as a result.

The newest TV deal for the English Premier League – the most lucrative yet – will create an even wider gulf between clubs in the top tier and the rest, with even the

FOOTBALL ON FILM

Footballers may be the closest modern equivalent to the Hollywood stars of the 1930s in terms of celebrity but football has until recently been peculiarly ill-served by the movies. Even the great John Huston – director of *The Maltese Falcon* and *Treasure of the Sierra Madre* – failed to work his magic on 1981's *Escape to Victory*, a ludicrous confection about Allied prisoners of war playing a Nazi Aryan superteam and escaping at the end of the match, though this movie does have a kitsch cult following that relishes the sight of Pele, Bobby Moore and Ossie Ardiles playing in front of Sylvester Stallone in goal. Given the sophisticated excellence of some US movies about baseball – *Field of Dreams*, *The Natural* and John Sayles' *Eight Men Out*, for example – you might assume football films have suffered from Hollywood's simple incomprehension of the game and what people love about it.

But British films about football have often been little better. Among the notable duds are *When Saturday Come*s, with Sean Bean leaving it a bit late in life to be plausibly playing for his boyhood team Sheffield United. Nick Hornby's brilliant *Fever Pitch*, the first book to understand passionate football support from the inside, was sadly let down by its pallid feature-film version, despite the presence of a post-Darcy Colin Firth. The best football moments have tended to be in films concerned with something else entirely, such as Ken Loach's *Kes* and Bill Forsyth's *Gregory's Gir*l, and even the enjoyable *Bend It Like*

Beckham derives all its life and verve from the Indian family setting rather than the fantasy football.

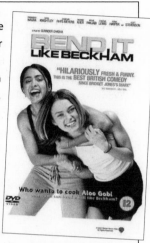

In the globalized, corporate era of modern professional football, however, Hollywood has now made its move, in a film trilogy featuring an inevitable walk-on part for David Beckham. 2006's *Goal!* was a rags-to-riches Latino fairy story but at least made significant efforts at football plausibility by spending months with Newcastle United, and recruited scriptwriters who understand the culture in *Likely Lads* creators Dick Clement and Ian La Frenais. In 2007's *Goal II* young Santiago moves to Real Madrid and in 2008's third instalment he will win the World Cup, though whether for Mexico or Argentina is as yet unclear. Why? Because the Mexican national team (the more obvious choice for a Latino from Los Angeles) was sponsored by Nike at the 2006 World Cup whereas the *Goal!* trilogy is exclusive to Adidas (who sponsor Argentina). Mexico have now seen the light and moved to Adidas, though maybe not in time to be immortalized on celluloid. The background sponsorship wrangles say more about modern football than the filmed sequences ever could. ◆

bottom-placed club receiving £25 million ($50 million).

Within each of the top leagues, however, power and wealth is increasingly concentrated in the hands of the few clubs with access to the megabucks guaranteed by participation in the latter stages of the UEFA Champions League. In England this has led to the emergence of a Big Four – Manchester United, Chelsea, Liverpool and Arsenal – that have effectively commandeered the Champions League places. With every passing season of burgeoning income, the harder it becomes for the clubs below them to compete, and other teams, with little chance of honors or glory, are often reduced to competing simply to avoid relegation.

In Italy and Spain the concentration of wealth has, if anything, been even more extreme, largely because the biggest clubs – Juventus, AC Milan, Internazionale, Real Madrid and FC Barcelona – have negotiated their own exclusive TV deals.

The money-making juggernaut seems unstoppable, and hitherto its effect has undeniably been to improve the standard of football in Europe – while impoverishing the standards almost everywhere else. The lucrative rewards on offer in the big leagues of western Europe have ensured that the best players from Latin America,

Africa and Asia all migrate to play there. This increases the attractiveness of those leagues to sponsors, advertisers and TV executives, all of whom can reach global audiences. But it means that the quality of professional football even in core countries with great traditions such as Brazil and Argentina has been drastically reduced, with attendances suffering as a result and the footballing public more interested in the outcome of matches in Europe (often featuring their local players) than of those in their home city.

FOOTBALL BETTING IN THE FAR EAST

Gambling is illegal virtually everywhere in the Far East, yet the betting industry there is worth $100 billion. European football is a favorite arena for these underground gamblers, with around $150 million bet on the results of matches on an average weekend. During the Euro 2004 tournament Thais gambled $800 million in three weeks while Singaporeans spent $294 million (an average of $70 per head of population).

This has led to allegations of match-fixing of games in Europe. In the late 1990s three Premiership games had to be postponed because the floodlights had been sabotaged by men attached to Asian gambling syndicates – the score in an abandoned game stands according to betting rules in Indonesia and Malaysia. ◆

Players cash in

Despite all this talk of money, it remains the case that all but the top clubs struggle to turn a profit, mainly because so much of their money is eaten up by players' salaries. At the outset of the English Premiership around half clubs' income went on paying players but by 2002 this had risen to two-thirds, while in Germany and Spain it was closer to 80 per cent and in Italy a staggering 90 per cent. European Union rulings on freedom of contract have allowed players to negotiate phenomenal salaries. The average annual salary in the Premiership in 2006 was £676,000 ($1.3 million), meaning players were earning in two weeks what the average fan could earn in a year. The top players, meanwhile – such as Wayne Rooney and Steven Gerrard – now earn more than £100,000 ($200,000) a week or $10 million a year – and that is without including their income from sponsorship or advertising, which can sometimes be in excess of that.

As these numbers suggest, the money received by players has ceased to bear any relation to normal life. It has led to absurdities such as Michael Owen being signed by Newcastle from Real Madrid, being injured before he could play a game for the club and proceeding to receive $200,000 a week all season while he recuperated. Even this, however, is not as absurd as the story of Winston Bogarde, a Dutch player signed by Chelsea from Barcelona, who spent four years at the club on a salary of £40,000 ($80,000 at current rates) yet played only 12

TOP-EARNING FOOTBALLERS IN 2006

(including salaries and sponsorship etc)

1 Ronaldinho (Barcelona / Brazil) – $29.5 million

2 David Beckham (Real Madrid / England) – $29.1 million

3 Ronaldo (AC Milan / Brazil) – $23.4 million

4 Wayne Rooney (Manchester United / England)
   – $17.2 million

5 Michael Ballack (Chelsea / Germany) – $16.8 million

6 Thierry Henry (Arsenal / France) – $15.8 million

7 Zinedine Zidane (Real Madrid / France) – $15.6 million

8 Fabio Cannavaro (Real Madrid / Italy) – $14.6 million

9 John Terry (Chelsea / England) – $14.3 million

10 Steven Gerrard (Liverpool / England) – $14.2 million

Source: Forbes

Ronaldinho
(Barcelona/Brazil).

games – not rated by his manager, he did not even sit on the substitutes' bench, yet no club could afford to take him off Chelsea's hands.

The galacticos and the Beckham factor

Ronaldinho's presence at the top of the chart on the previous page is a touch ironic. Few could have argued that in 2006 he was the best player in the world – his sinuous skill had done much to make FC Barcelona European champions and even more to show the game at its beautiful, inspiring best. Yet he was notoriously ignored by Real Madrid, whose strategy in the last decade has involved the collection of 'galácticos' – the world's best and most marketable individuals. When asked why the club had not pursued the famously bucktoothed Ronaldinho, a director said: 'There was no point in buying him, it wasn't worth it. He is so ugly that he'd sink you as a brand.'

The epitome of the 'galáctico' approach – and indeed of this phase of globalized, commercialized football – has been the English right midfielder David Beckham (pictured facing page), signed by Real Madrid from Manchester United in 2003. If footballers are now more effective than movie stars in promoting most types of merchandise, Beckham embodies modern celebrity – his individual fame reaches the parts that no footballer has ever dreamed of reaching before. Gifted player though he certainly is, this celebrity has been based far less on his footballing achievements than on his good looks and his personal style, as well as his crossover into pop music culture via his ex-Spice Girl wife Victoria.

An index of Beckham's global power came when his face appeared on billboards in Tehran in 2003 advertising engine oil but was swiftly covered up by the

Islamic regime. Why? Beckham has become the poster-boy for the Western consumerist lifestyle that so appalls the mullahs, his every change of hairstyle a slap in the face for strict religious observance. They may also have considered him to be too dangerously imbued with sexuality: a 2007 poll saw Beckham's body voted the second most envied male body on the planet, second only to film star Brad Pitt's.

When Beckham concluded a deal to move to the Los Angeles Galaxy from 2007 on a $250-million five-year deal, it seemed to many an appropriate swansong given that his image has always been far closer in spirit to the sun-soaked Hollywood hills than to the rain-drenched environs of Manchester.

THE RICH LIST

Club income during 2005-2006 (in millions of euros)

1 Real Madrid (Spain) 292.2
2 Barcelona (Spain) 259.1
3 Juventus (Italy) 251.2
4 Manchester United (England) 242.6
5 AC Milan (Italy) 238.7
6 Chelsea (England) 221.0
7 Internazionale (Italy) 206.6
8 Bayern München (Germany) 204.7
9 Arsenal (England) 192.4
10 Liverpool (England) 176.0
11 Lyon (France) 127.7
12 Roma (Italy) 127.0
13 Newcastle United (England) 124.3
14 Schalke 04 (Germany) 122.9
15 Tottenham Hotspur (England) 107.2
16 Hamburg (Germany) 101.8
17 Manchester City (England) 89.4
18 Glasgow Rangers (Scotland) 88.5
19 West Ham United (England) 60.1
20 Benfica (Portugal) 58.8

Real Madrid badge.

Gamekeepers turned poachers

The vast changes in global football have been reflected in the body that runs the international game, the Fédération Internationale de Football Association (FIFA).

FIFA was founded in 1904 in Paris, and originally did not include any of the national associations in Britain, which considered that they were so far ahead of the rest of the world that they did not deign to participate – as late as 1938 the British were so insular and had such an inflated sense of their own superiority that they did not bother to enter the World Cup.

Until 1974 FIFA was a tiny organization with little ambition and next to no money, which existed to look after the rules of the game and to organize one tournament every four years. Its president from 1961 was an English former goalkeeper, teacher, referee and FA secretary, Sir Stanley Rous, who worked unpaid in the role as a retirement interest. A relative modernizer and Europhile within the English game, he was largely incapable of dealing with the postcolonial footballing world – 31 newly independent African countries joined FIFA between 1958 and 1967, yet Africa was offered just a play-off with Asia's champions for a single place at the 1966 World Cup finals (they boycotted the qualifying competition in

MATCH-FIXING: NOT JUST AN ITALIAN PROBLEM

Football in the northern summer of 2006 was in danger of descending into farce. Italy rather unexpectedly won its fourth World Cup in Germany while it was in the midst of one of its greatest footballing scandals, known as *Calciopoli*. In May 2006 police reported that transcripts of telephone conversations revealed officials at some of the country's top clubs to have been involved in match-fixing, specifically by influencing referees, or by ensuring that referees favoring them were allocated to particular games.

The Italian champions Juventus – long suspected of fixing games – were the main offenders. They were stripped of their 2005 and 2006 titles and relegated. Fiorentina and Lazio were originally threatened with relegation but escaped with points deductions; AC Milan narrowly escaped losing its place in the Champions League for 2006-07, a competition it was eventually to win.

Match-fixing is by no means a new phenomenon. Here are just a few examples:

1915 Manchester United, threatened with relegation, beat Liverpool 2-0. The match is fixed by players on both sides anxious to benefit from a betting scam before they lose their livelihood due to the First World War.

1971 The president of Hertha Berlin, a club already relegated partly for bribing opposing players, launches a crusade to prove how widespread bribery and match-fixing is in the rest of the German Bundesliga. At least two-thirds of the league's clubs are eventually implicated and 50 players, coaches and club presidents receive life bans.

1994 A year after winning the Champions League, Marseille are found guilty of corruption and match-fixing and are relegated from the French first division.

1996 Ridiculous results on the final day of the Polish season result in the punishment of both Legia Warsaw and ŁKS Łódz (already guilty of match-fixing three years before).

2000 Roma's president is found to have given a Rolex watch worth $20,000 to every Serie A referee.

2002 In Romania it is revealed that for a decade a dozen top clubs have been operating a cartel guaranteeing home wins where necessary in order to ensure they are not relegated. In Greece tapes played on a radio show expose a conspiracy involving match-fixing by referees, club-owners and officials but no punishments have ensued.

2004-2006 Criminal investigations and trials related to match-fixing take place in Italy, Portugal, Greece, the Czech Republic, Belgium, the Netherlands, Finland, Poland and Germany.

2005 The *Escândalo do Apito* in Brazil sees FIFA referee Edílson Pereira de Carvalho found guilty of rigging matches on behalf of a betting syndicate. Eleven matches refereed by him have to be replayed. ◆

protest). South Africa was his particular Achilles' heel – he traveled to the country in 1963 and reported that its exclusively white governing body – rather than other 'dissident' federations that involved black people – was the only possible affiliate to FIFA.

Rous was defeated in a presidential election by João Havelange, an entrepreneur who had been president of the Brazilian football confederation (CBF). His ace card was his promise to expand the World Cup and offer more places to Africa – and winning the FIFA presidency proved to be a stroke of immense good fortune for Havelange because just as he took up the post the CBF discovered that over six million dollars had vanished from the organization during his term of office. The country's military rulers considered putting Havelange on trial but decided that would be too embarrassing given his international status and so made up the missing funds by taking it out of the social welfare budget.

Havelange immediately set about completely transforming FIFA. Together with Horst Dassler (son of Adi Dassler, the founder of Adidas) and sports marketing specialist Patrick Nally, he turned the World Cup into a cash cow, capitalizing on global television rights and corporate sponsorship by the biggest transnationals –

beginning with a deal signed with Coca-Cola in 1975.

Spain in 1982 was the first World Cup completely under Havelange's control – the first with the expanded format of 24 teams – and he ensured that the money poured in. Nobody knows just how much money FIFA wades around in – its finances and its corporate deals have always been wreathed in secrecy. But Havelange himself drew out at least a million dollars in expenses each year and by the 1990s FIFA had a gleaming new headquarters housing more than 100 full-time staff.

TV viewing figures for the World Cup rose exponentially. In Africa in the early 1970s there were under a million TVs – but there were 20 million by 1990, by which point there were a billion sets all over the world. And as the TV viewing figures expanded, so too did the money from corporations anxious to push their products to the most global of all captive audiences.

It was, it must be said, an inspired business plan. And it was one that made Havelange something like an untouchable god. A FIFA executive member said of him: 'He is everywhere... heaven and hell, like the Pope.' The Swiss football federation, shamefully desperate for the chance to stage the 1998 World Cup, even had the gall to nominate him for the Nobel Peace Prize.

FOOTBALL THROUGH THE LOOKING GLASS

Many things in the world are badly governed. There are many élites who are incompetent, self-serving, self-important and arrogantly blasé about their evident limitations. None of them can begin to compare with the circus masquerading as the global governance of football. Sepp Blatter's first eight years in power make one nostalgic for the authoritarian certainties, the despicable charm and haughty, patrician discretion of the Havelange years.

At the level of everyday management and internal politics, Blatter's regime has been a disgrace. From the very start of his reign he attempted to create new circuits of bureaucratic power among his hand-picked staff and within the presidential office. The conduct of FIFA business, always an opulent intercontinental affair, has spiraled to the levels of the grotesque. The massively enlarged carbuncle of football bureaucrats on FIFA business, deliberately created by Blatter as a phalanx of kept support, have lived the high life. In addition to the five-star hotels, the business-class flights, the black Mercedes, they have all been allowed a daily expenses rate of $500 for which no receipts or records are required. Members of the executive committee were handed $50,000 honorariums and President Blatter's salary, emoluments, expenses and accounts remain, despite repeated requests from the press and UEFA, a matter of complete secrecy...

At the FIFA executive committee meeting in May 2002 the general secretary Michel Zen-Ruffinen blew the whistle, making and distributing statements outlining in depth the scale and scope of mismanagement within the organization. So detailed and comprehensive was the account that 11 members of the FIFA executive committee lodged a criminal complaint based on its contents to the Swiss public prosecutor's office in Zurich, including 13 specific cases of unaccountable financial transactions. The day before the vote [Cameroonian Issa Hayatou was challenging Blatter for the presidency], an extraordinary congress was held to investigate and air all the grievances and accusations concerning FIFA's finances...

In an open, amateurish display of micro-political bullying, obfuscation and filibustering, the day was filled with long paeans of praise to Blatter and incoherent criticism of his opponents from football association presidents closely bound to the Blatter camp. Critics from within the executive were not given any space to speak... Adam Crozier, the head of the English FA, described it as 'an absolute disgrace from start to finish. There was no attempt at transparency in two hours of manipulation.' When the votes rolled in the next day Blatter had won by an even bigger margin than in 1998, 139 to 56. When Leo Mugabe, nephew of Robert Mugabe and dictatorial president of the Zimbabwean Football Federation, could comment, 'It is shocking – this is a travesty of democracy,' then one has reached a moral ground zero. ◆

David Goldblatt *The Ball Is Round:*
A Global History of Football (Viking 2006)

João Havelange and Sepp Blatter pictured in 2006.

Havelange's reign – and the word is more appropriate than 'term of office' given the opulence and the utter lack of accountability involved in the role of FIFA President – came to an end at the 1998 World Cup. His successor had been his henchman throughout his time in power – a Swiss lawyer called Sepp Blatter. And if Havelange's high-handedness and 'creative' approach to matters financial was extraordinary, Blatter's behavior since has been mind-boggling (see box, pages 76-77).

It is no exaggeration to say that Sepp Blatter is a laughing stock. His ideas about football – including banning drawn games, widening the goals and holding a

World Cup every two years – are almost always dismissed as ridiculous. His considered opinion on women's football, which is growing in participation and popularity all over the world, was: 'Let the women play in more feminine clothes like they do in volleyball. They could, for example, have tighter shorts.'

Such idiocies might be merely amusing were it not for Blatter's unaccountable wealth and power. His continued presence at the pinnacle of the world game is shameful. It is evident to more or less anyone who comments on football or who holds its best interests at heart that Blatter must be replaced by someone prepared to clean the Augean stables, someone who will bring transparency, financial probity and even a modicum of ethical awareness to FIFA's operations. Yet Blatter, who had previously said he would retire after his second term, was returned unopposed to the presidency in 2007 and will now serve in the global game's most prominent post until 2011. What a bizarre world we live in.

4 Politics and the ball

'Football, metaphor for war, at times turns into real war. Then "sudden death" is no longer just a dramatic way of deciding a tied match. These days, football fanaticism has come to occupy the place formerly reserved for religious fervor, patriotic ardor and political passion. As often occurs with religion, patriotism and politics, football can bring tensions to a boil, and many horrors are committed in its name.'
EDUARDO GALEANO

Football, then, has become an important leisure interest and entertainment industry all over the world. But what has that to do with the real, serious world of hard news and politics, human rights and warfare?

You might be surprised how many points of contact

there have always been. Ever since it became evident that football engaged the passions of the mass public, politicians of all shades and stripes have sought to co-opt it and harness its appeal to their own ends – those that did not, like Mao's regime during the Cultural Revolution and Ayatollah Khomeini's in the first flood of Iranian theocracy, attempt to ban it.

For Kwame Nkrumah (pictured), first leader of independent Ghana, football was much more than just a game – it was a demonstration of Africa's immense potential. He celebrated independence by arranging a tour of Ghana by the English winger Stanley Matthews, famed for his extraordinary dribbling. But this was merely a means to the end of developing an African team that could compete on the world stage. Nkrumah was the apostle of Pan-Africanism rather than nationalism, but that did not stop him wanting to win. He joined up Ghana to the nascent African football confederation (CAF)

immediately after independence in 1957 and soon arranged to host the 1963 African Cup of Nations. In preparation for the tournament he called the national team the Black Stars – named after the boat chartered in 1922 by Marcus Garvey to bring black Americans back to Africa – and poured resources into their improvement, arranging tours to Europe in 1962 and early 1963 that included a victory over Italy.

Ghana beat Sudan in the final and won again in Tunisia two years later. In that sense they showed what was possible, demonstrating that Africans given their independent head could achieve things that had been considered impossible under colonialism. But by then the early Pan-African idealism was beginning to sour – the CAF may not have been the most efficient operation in the world but as an exercise in African co-operation it came a great deal closer to embodying Pan-Africanism than the new Organization of African Unity, set up in 1963. By the time of Ghana's second Cup victory, Nkrumah was ruling a one-party state at home in an increasingly authoritarian manner and he was ousted in a military coup in 1966, setting a precedent for the African politics of the next three decades that he would have hated to contemplate.

Mobutu's leopards

One of the primary exemplars of that kind of politics was a leader without a shred of Nkrumah's idealism but who learned from his football experiment – Mobutu Sese Seko

of Zaire (now Democratic Republic of Congo). Ghana's Black Stars toured Zaire in 1966, the year after Mobutu had come to power in a coup, and he was inspired by their example to invest some of the wealth and power he was already accruing in his own national team. He took over the football authorities, appointed a Yugoslav as coach and arranged for Zairean professionals playing in Belgium to come home.

At first it was another success story: Zaire won the 1968 African Cup of Nations in Addis Ababa and the team received a rapturous welcome on their return to Kinshasa. Mobutu started calling them the Leopards instead of the Lions, in ludicrous tribute to his own leopardskin hat. The team had become a symbol of his own 'greatness' – his kleptomaniac dictatorial rule had now tumbled into megalomania. Not only did they win the tournament again in 1974, they also qualified for the World Cup finals in West Germany later that year.

But there the fairy story ended with a thud – Zaire were not only beaten in all three of their games but were embarrassingly trounced, 9-0, by Yugoslavia. With typical bad grace, Mobutu immediately disavowed any further interest in football and let it be known that the players were to be cold-shouldered. On their return, there was not even a bus to meet them, let alone a welcoming committee, and they continued to be treated like lepers throughout Mobutu's long rule. Mobutu had moved on to his next whim – hosting the famous fight between Muhammad Ali and George Foreman in Kinshasa, the so-called 'Rumble in the Jungle'.

More recently Nigeria's President, Olusegun Obasanjo, has played midfield in a grudge match between the Federal Executive and the Legislature, which had been disputing the size of the federal budget for months. Obasanjo's team won 1-0 with a goal by the President himself and you have to wonder exactly how committed the opposing defenders and goalkeeper were able to be in such circumstances. As, indeed, when Ugandan President Yoweri Museveni led a joint cabinet-parliament side to a 2-1 victory against the local football association.

Perhaps surprisingly, a footballer's attempt to travel in the opposite direction came to grief in 2005. George Weah was a gifted Liberian striker who achieved fame and fortune in the European game – mainly for Monaco, Paris Saint-Germain and AC Milan – and was the first African to win the World Footballer of the Year award in

WORLD CUP WINNERS

It remains a peculiarity that European nations have never won a World Cup outside Europe, while only Brazil of the Latin American nations has won outside the Americas. This is a trend unlikely to continue given the increased globalization of the game and the concentration of the world's best players in the major European leagues.

Year	Winner	Location
1930	Uruguay	Uruguay
1934	Italy	Italy
1938	Italy	France
1950	Uruguay	Brazil
1954	West Germany	Switzerland
1958	Brazil	Sweden
1962	Brazil	Chile
1966	England	England
1970	Brazil	Mexico
1974	West Germany	West Germany
1978	Argentina	Argentina
1982	Italy	Spain
1986	Argentina	Mexico
1990	Germany	Italy
1994	Brazil	United States
1998	France	France
2002	Brazil	Japan/South Korea
2006	Italy	Germany

1995. Long known for his humanitarian work – he was for many years a UNICEF Goodwill Ambassador – he stood in the first presidential election following the country's long and bitter civil war but lost out to Ellen Johnson-Sirleaf, an academic who became Africa's first elected female head of state.

Saddam's sick son

Arguably the worst football administrator of all time was also a politician: Uday Hussein, son of Saddam, who was handed control of both Iraq's Football Association and its Olympic Committee in 1984. Uday began by creating his own club, Al-Rasheed, for which he commandeered all the best players in the country. Not content with this, he 'consulted' with referees in advance about Al-Rasheed's games, with the inevitable result that the club won three national titles in succession.

The fear engendered by Uday was entirely understandable because he did not restrict himself to mere empty threats – though he was pretty free with those, as when he told the national team that he would blow their plane up if they lost a match abroad. When the team failed to qualify for the 1994 World Cup finals, Uday forced them to kick concrete footballs until most of the bones in their feet were broken.

Sharar Hayday, one of the players in the national squad, remembers: 'I was tortured four times after matches. One time after a friendly against Jordan in Amman that we lost 2-0, Uday had me and three team-mates taken to prison. When we arrived they took off our shirts, tied our feet together and pulled our knees over a bar as we lay on our backs. Then they dragged us over pavement and concrete, pulling the skin off our backs. Then they dragged us through a sandpit to get sand in our backs. Finally, they made us climb a ladder and jump into a vat of raw sewage.'

Serbia's shock troops

Violence has been an unfortunate adjunct to the game ever since it became a major spectator sport, though more normally it involves clashes between rival football fans. These range from the sectarian conflict between Rangers and Celtic fans in Glasgow to the *barras bravas* groups in Latin America, from the *torcidas* in Brazil to the *teppisti* who rioted in Catania, Sicily, and caused the death of a police officer in February 2007.

Only in former Yugoslavia, however, have football 'hooligans' become organized mass murderers. The first open warfare between Serbs and Croats came at a football match between Red Star Belgrade and Dinamo Zagreb in 1990, just after the election of the ultranationalist Croat leader Franjo Tudjman, which turned into a full-scale battle on the pitch between rival fans. Present on the Serbian side was a notorious gangster and secret  police assassin known as Zeljko Raznatovic, better known as Arkan (pictured), to whom Slobodan Milosevic's interior minister had given the job of channeling the violent tendencies of Red Star's most brutish male fans.

When the Yugoslav civil war began in earnest, Arkan's football shock troops transmuted into a paramilitary group called the Tigers, taking their soccer songs with them to the front. Their specialty was 'ethnic cleansing' – terrorizing and murdering Croat or Bosnian Muslim civilians. By the end of the civil war, Arkan's Tigers had summarily executed at least 2,000 people and Arkan himself had become a bizarre national hero, marrying the pop star Ceca live on TV in 1994.

That was by no means the end of Arkan's football connections. In post-war Serbia the Tigers became a sanctions-breaking blackmarket business operation, making Arkan millions in the process. He used the money to buy his own football club, Obilic (named after a knight in the 1389 Battle of Kosovo), and made the tiger the club symbol. Success came immediately – promotion to the top division was followed the very next year by a national championship. Small wonder – referees were 'escorted' to games by armed Tigers, opposition players were threatened with murder by fans who often waved guns and one was even locked in a garage so that he could not play.

The following season, the other clubs decided to take a firm collective stand. Arkan reined in the intimidation and Obilic faded back into obscurity. In January 2000 Arkan himself was shot dead by person or persons unknown in the lobby of Belgrade's Intercontinental Hotel.

Up the junta

In the sorry intersection of politics and football, there are few stories more shameful than the 1978 World Cup in Argentina. The generals took over in Argentina in March 1976 after an admittedly woeful and increasingly conflict-ridden period of civilian, though often authoritarian, rule. They had three priorities: hunting down 'subversives' and leftists of all kinds; turning the economy over to the free market; and getting ready for the World Cup. The tournament had been awarded to the country as long ago as 1964 but next to nothing had been accomplished in the intervening 12 years: none of the new stadiums had been built; none of the new transport and communications infrastructure was in place.

If there is a single positive thing to be said about the Argentinean generals, it can only be that they made the World Cup trains run on time. This got off to a bizarre start, however. General Omar Actis was appointed World Cup tsar, responsible for getting things moving, only to be assassinated at his very first press conference. Though leftists were inevitably blamed, it is rumored that the assassination was ordered by his successor as tsar, Carlos Alberto Lacoste, an Admiral who strangely combined the name of Brazil's 1970 World Cup-winning captain and France's first tennis star and sports apparel designer. Lacoste duly got the stadiums and the roads built, to hell with the cost – and managed to build into every contract due consideration for his own future bank balance and pension.

All this expenditure and public works went hand in glove with savage cuts in all other forms of public spending or social support; unemployment soared and economic hardship mounted. But even this paled into insignificance beside the dictatorship's vicious repression. The initial focus on eradicating the Montoneros and EPZ guerrillas very quickly expanded to include the rounding up, torture and 'disappearance' of thousands of leftists, students and union officials – an estimated 30,000 by the end of military rule in 1983.

Surely the World Cup could not be played under such conditions? Human-rights groups and Argentinean exiles campaigned for a boycott but FIFA barely gave a thought to the idea of playing the tournament elsewhere. Some nations, notably Holland, were more receptive to the idea but ultimately went with the flow – with the honorable

exception of the Dutch star player, Johann Cruyff, who refused to travel on principle. The generals were rewarded not only with the incomparable PR of a tournament that went off smoothly but with the dream result of Argentina's first World Cup win (and over pinko-sympathizing Holland in the final to boot); TV pictures were beamed

Mario Kempes scoring for Argentina in the 1978 World Cup final.

THE TORTURE STADIUM

Anyone not expecting the international football authorities to cut such a shameful figure as they did in Argentina in 1978 had not been paying attention just five years earlier. Chile was then going through its own nightmare period of military dictatorship following General Augusto Pinochet's overthrow of President Allende's democratically elected socialist government. Activists and 'potential troublemakers' of all kinds were rounded up, at least 12,000 of them 'processed' in the National Stadium in Santiago, which had once hosted the 1962 World Cup Final but now acted as a torture chamber. Just four days after the coup, Chile played the Soviet Union in Moscow in a play-off – the winners over two legs would qualify for the 1974 World Cup. The second leg was scheduled to take place two months later in the very stadium where human rights atrocities were taking place.

The Soviets appealed to FIFA to move the game to another venue and were backed by many national associations in Africa and Asia. A FIFA delegation was taken on a sanitized tour by the Chilean regime and obligingly gave the stadium a clean bill of health. The Soviet Union saw no alternative but to pull out of the game, sending FIFA a telegram of no mean dignity saying 'Soviet sportsmen cannot at present play at stadium stained with the blood of Chilean patriots'. They were duly disqualified. East Germany wrote to FIFA's English President, Sir Stanley Rous, asking if he would hold a football match inside Dachau. ◆

all over the world of General Videla presenting the trophy to national captain Daniel Passarella in front of 70,000 delirious fans.

Kicking out the colonists

But these are thoroughly negative examples – surely football must somewhere, somehow, have served as a positive influence on political change?

In Algeria football can certainly be said to have played its part in the cause of liberation. Then a French colony, Algeria's nationalist aspirations gained in strength after the Second World War. At first football was just a convenient rallying-ground – nationalist chants in football stadiums, increasing violence by crowds against the French police. The cause of Algerian nationalism hit the headlines in France when former president of the Algerian assembly Ali Chekkal – an opponent of independence – was assassinated in the VIP box at the French Cup Final in 1957.

The rebel National Liberation Front (FLN), which had announced its armed struggle for independence in Switzerland while the 1954 World Cup finals were being played there, then achieved a huge footballing coup. The top Algerian footballers of the day inevitably played

 in France and the best of them, Rachid Mekloufi (pictured), won the World Military Games title with the French Army team in 1957. He was all set to play for France at the 1958 World Cup. Instead, he and eight other Algerian professional footballers traveled secretly to Tunis to form the official team of the FLN government-in-exile.

This hit the French public much harder than all the tales of Algerian politicians going underground to wage war for independence. Over the next four years Mekloufi and his team played with great brio all over the Arab and Communist world, serving as admirable ambassadors for their cause. When the bitter war of independence was finally won in 1962, however, Mekloufi remarkably returned to France to play – and was welcomed by all but right-wing colonialist diehards. As captain of St Etienne, Mekloufi stepped up to receive the French Cup from President Charles de Gaulle, who had overseen France's inglorious withdrawal from its former colony. De Gaulle presented the trophy with the ambiguous words 'La France, c'est vous'. The words may be thought to anticipate by more than three decades France's half-delighted, half-shocked discovery in 1998 that it was now a rainbow nation, with a World Cup-winning football team half made up of players descended from its various (ex-)colonies or other countries.

The quintessential football politician

Nobody understands the potential political power of football better than Italy's Silvio Berlusconi. Initially a property developer, Berlusconi gained an interest in cable TV through its installation in the luxurious gated communities he built in Milan, and seized the chance to build his own channel, zeroing in on the lowest common denominator with wall-to-wall Hollywood imports, cartoons, cruddy gameshows – and football, as much of it as he could get. Presenting himself as a crusader for ordinary people's interests, he bought up all his competitors and managed to overturn legislation that barred any cable channels from broadcasting nationally. He celebrated in 1986 by taking over AC Milan, then languishing in the doldrums having been disgraced and relegated for its part in the match-fixing *totocalcio* scandal of 1980.

You had to hand it to Berlusconi – he thought big. The first appearance of AC Milan under his new ownership involved the team arriving at the San Siro stadium in helicopters to the rousing strains of Wagner's *Ride of the Valkyries* – a shameless echo of the scene in Francis Ford Coppola's 1979 Vietnam War film *Apocalypse Now*. In this case, however, pride did not presage a fall: Berlusconi showed considerable footballing vision, making good managerial appointments, funding inspired transfers – notably the Dutch maestros Ruud Gullit, Marco van Basten and Frank Rijkaard – and insisting on bravura attacking football that confounded the safety-first culture of Italian tradition. In 1988 they won the Italian league title, the *scudetto*, and the following year played magnificently and memorably to win the European Cup, beating Real Madrid 5-0 in the semi-final and sweeping past Steua Bucharest 4-0 in the final.

Not content with this – or with another European Cup in 1990, or indeed with the longest unbeaten run in the history of Italy's top division, Serie A (58 games between 1992 and 1994) – Berlusconi moved into politics. As he saw it, his hand was forced. In the early 1990s much of the political élite had been disgraced and charged with corruption and embezzlement, including many of his closest cronies. A political vacuum was opening up that might well be filled by the new Party of the Democratic Left and threaten his ever-more monstrous business interests.

He described the situation in impeccable footballing terms: 'I heard that things were getting dangerous, and that it was all being played in the penalty area, with the midfield being left desolately empty.'

His answer was to form his own party in 1993, Forza Italia, itself named after the fans' chant for the national team. The party made unashamed use of AC Milan supporters' clubs up and down the country as well as Berlusconi's media outlets and managed to win 21 per cent of the vote in the 1994 election. Drawing allies from the new parties of the Right, which included many politicians with dubious neo-fascist views and connections, Berlusconi was asked to form a government. In a storyline that would not have been believable in the trashiest of dramas on his TV channels, the vital vote in parliament that made him Prime Minister took place on the same night, 18 May 1994, as AC Milan were thrashing FC Barcelona 4-0 to take the European Champions League title.

Iran's women fans

Football was vigorously promoted by Iran's last two Shahs – as a key part of Westernization by Reza Shah between the wars, and then by his son, himself a passionate player and supporter of the game, in the 1950s and 1960s. If there was a single moment when football became the nation's game it was when the national team beat Israel 2-1 in the Asian Nations Cup in the immediate aftermath of the 1967 Arab-Israeli Six-Day War.

When the Islamic Revolution brought the Shah's downfall in 1979, Ayatollah Khomeini's first impulse was to repress football out of existence in the same way as all other perceived Western cultural impositions such as pop music. But it soon became evident that this would probably be impossible, and that the unpopularity that would result from a ban would endanger its other initiatives. For a while it tried instead to co-opt football, starting pro-government chants in the stadiums – only for its cheerleaders to be laughed out.

Now Iran's rulers content themselves with filtering out unsavory influences – broadcasting matches with a slight delay, for instance, so as to remove any obscene or subversive chanting, and blotting out the sponsors' logos on the shirts of players in photographs of foreign matches.

But some things the regime cannot control. Iran's top players, for instance, most of whom inevitably ply their trade abroad, have a conspicuous lack of suitably Islamic beards and have become romantic figures and cultural icons. When the national team plays, the nation stops to watch – and that includes many of the nation's women.

Women were forbidden from watching football from the earliest days of the Revolution – the sight of men's legs, apart from anything else, was considered deeply unsuitable. But such was the passion of the top clerics' daughters that Khomeini was eventually prevailed upon to issue a modifying *fatwa* – in 1987 he ruled that women could now watch football on TV, though they could still not attend it live.

By 1997, Khomeini was long gone but the rule still held. The national team then won a play-off with Australia on away goals to qualify for the 1998 World Cup finals and the people erupted on to the streets. In the comfortable suburbs, particularly, young women joined men celebrating and even threw off their required hair coverings in gay abandon.

The regime pleaded for restraint when the victorious team arrived home from Australia, urging all women to stay at home. The team-members were flown by helicopter into the massive Azadi ('Freedom') Stadium in the center of Tehran.

Iranian football supporters watching the national team on TV during the 2006 World Cup.

Thousands of women gathered outside the stadium, chanting to be let in, using words like: 'Aren't we part of this nation? We want to celebrate too. We aren't ants.' To avoid trouble, the police allowed 3,000 of the women into special segregated seats. But the remaining 2,000 were still frozen out and, far from accepting their exclusion, burst past the turnstiles into the main body of the stadium. The police accepted defeat.

The issue was revived when Iran played Ireland in another World Cup play-off in 2001 and 20 Irish women were allowed into the Azadi Stadium to watch. The evident discrimination against Iranian women caused a furore in media that had been loosened by reformist President Khatami. Eventually, in 2003, women were experimentally allowed to attend a suburban game, in a special area of the stands.

But when President Ahmadinejad proposed something similar in the run-up to the 2006 World Cup – an unusually enlightened move by the hardliner – he was howled down by the leading clerics. Faced with such intransigence, some women even take the risk of dressing in male clothing in order to be able to infiltrate stadiums for matches – a practice highlighted in the recent Iranian feature film *Offside*, by Jafar Panahi. Needless to say, the movie was banned inside Iran.

Japan needs you, football

In football, as in so many things, Japan is a case apart. Just as the country completely recreated itself in the late 19th century, successfully moving from medieval isolation to industrialization in the space of a generation, so it more or less willed itself into being as a footballing nation.

The nation's preference had been for baseball. This was not just a reflection of US economic and cultural influence: it is a game well suited to Japan's rigid hierarchical culture, in that it involves disciplined teams follow the instructions of senior coaches to the letter.

But in the 1980s the Japanese economy hit big trouble. The old industries that had served it so well were faltering and it was clear that Japan needed to embrace the coming,

A Japanese football magazine.

fluid, globalized economy built on services. The old deferential culture no longer seemed so appropriate.

Football may be a team game in which a coach picks the team and decides tactics but it flows endlessly and unpredictably. Players have to be aware of collective needs and duties but they also cannot function unless they can take individual responsibility and express their own spontaneity and creativity. Of all the world's games, football seemed most conducive to nurturing a new Japanese way of operating in the world.

In the late 1980s the decision was therefore taken to create a footballing culture. How could this be? Almost everywhere else in the world football spreads from the grassroots – the masses seize it from the privileged as soon as they encounter the wonders of its flow and fire.

In Japan, however, the game was reinvented from the top down. A professional league was launched in 1992 on the European model, comprising clubs with new names (no corporate names allowed), new stadiums and affiliations to their local communities.

European players and coaches were recruited – among them Arsène Wenger, later the highly successful manager of Arsenal, who said of his Japanese players: 'They wanted specific instructions from me. But football is not American football, where the coach can give instruction for each play... The player with the ball should be in charge of the game. I had to teach them to think for themselves.'

The footballing experiment has been a success. Japan co-hosted the 2002 World Cup with another country feeling its way out of a deferential, hierarchical cultural heritage, South Korea – and its national team acquitted itself entirely honorably. And given Japan's past achievements, who would bet against the wider cultural experiment also being successful? – though administrators have been given pause for thought by the unspeakably boorish behavior of some fans, copied from the incessant TV coverage of European games.

5 Can the beautiful game be reclaimed?

'"It is a game before a product, a sport before a market, a show before a business."
MICHEL PLATINI, UEFA PRESIDENT.

We should never forget that football's most important incarnation – kids (or grown-up kids) playing for fun, delighting in their own physical endeavor and skill, discovering the virtues of teamwork, or dreaming their dreams of glory as they practise in their own backyard – has changed very little over the past 50 years. But professional football has changed beyond the imagining of the players and supporters of the mid-20th century.

When I first started going regularly to Tottenham

games at the age of seven I used to travel by train and bus with two friends – and that we were allowed to go off on our own to join football crowds of up to 50,000 people in itself is redolent of a more trusting and more innocent age. We would arrive at the ground 90 minutes early so as to be first through the turnstiles (paying just one shilling and sixpence, which was probably around 20 US cents at the time) and stake our claim to the spot at the front closest to the pitch. Only the poshest people in those days had seats – the rest of us stood crammed together, often touched by our neighbors on all sides, and moving involuntarily as they did, straining our necks to see a corner or jumping in exultation as Jimmy Greaves (pictured) painted his latest masterpiece on the turf. This was more than just a shared community, it was like a living animal, sharing

its frustrations, delights and its sheer body warmth.

Standing terraces are still a part of football-watching all over the world but no longer at the highest level of the professional game: UEFA and FIFA insist that all matches under their control are played in all-seater stadiums. In general this is a safety issue – the all-seater requirement was legally enforced in England in the 1990s as a response to the Hillsborough disaster of 1989, in which 96 Liverpool fans were crushed to death. Football stadiums are also safer places to be in relation to violence between opposing fans – the advent of seated areas, more rigorous segregation and especially CCTV has successfully ensured that violence inside stadiums – something particularly associated with the English game in the 1970s and 1980s – is now a rarity. They are also less exclusively male, as many more women and girls than in the past have become hooked on the game.

But there is no question that something has been lost as well as gained. It is at least arguable that a seated audience is less engaged, more prepared to treat the game as pure spectacle. The ultimate expression of this is the modern 'executive box', wherein people are wined and dined while watching the game from behind glass. Former Liverpool manager Bill Shankly's famous adage (which no self-respecting football book could go to press without including) maybe doesn't apply any more to quite the same extent: 'Some people believe football is a matter of life and death: I am very disappointed with that attitude. I can assure you it is much, much more

BEAUTY TO DUTY

The history of football is a sad voyage from beauty to duty. When the sport became an industry, the beauty that blossoms from the joy of play got torn out by its very roots... Play has become spectacle, with few protagonists and many spectators, football for watching. And that spectacle has become one of the most profitable businesses in the world, organized not for play but rather to impede it. The technocracy of professional sport has managed to impose a football of lightning speed and brute strength, a football that negates joy, kills fantasy and outlaws daring.

Luckily, on the field you can still see, even if only once in a long while, some insolent rascal who sets aside the script and commits the blunder of dribbling past the entire opposing side, the referee and the crowd in the stands, all for the carnal delight of embracing the forbidden adventure of freedom. ◆

Eduardo Galeano, from *Football in Sun and Shadow*
(Fourth Estate 1997/2003).

important than that.'

Eduardo Galeano may sound jaundiced in the boxed extract above, but from the rest of his writing it is clear that although he deplores many things than have happened to the game, he is still as absorbed by it as he ever was. And I am much the same. I can rue the effect that television and its money have had on the game, for example, and remember with fondness the days when matches all kicked off at the same time on a Saturday afternoon. Yet I also naturally relish the fact that I can now see almost all Tottenham games, home and away, in some sort of televisual form.

The relationship between fans and players, however, has irrevocably changed. Until the 1960s in England players were paid only a little more than the average industrial wage. Even once the maximum wage had been overturned (in 1961) and players could bargain for much bigger sums of money, the rewards were not so extraordinary as to set them apart from the (mainly working-class) people they played for. Even England's 1966 World Cup-winning team comprised men not dissimilar in background or in approach to life from ordinary fans.

Money grows on trees

Today's footballers, in contrast, are sucked from early adolescence onwards into an alternative universe that bears no relation to the lives of ordinary people, where their every whim is gratified and money grows on trees. This has especially been true since the 1996 Bosman ruling, which used European law to dismantle previous controls, leading to rocketing players' salaries and allowing the richest clubs to sign up the best players.

The Brazilian striker Ronaldo's celebrity-packed 'engagement party' at the Chateau Chantilly, near Paris, in 2005 was symbolic of this transformation of footballers into a new aristocracy, as unashamed of their

NEW SLAVE TRADE

An investigation by *The Observer* last week found that Lebanese businessmen in Abidjan [capital of Côte d'Ivoire], an entrepreneurial community once preoccupied with diamond and timber smuggling, are turning their attention to football, establishing illegal training schools across the country in an attempt to farm the best talent out to some of the Middle East and Europe's largest clubs.

The children's parents and the youngsters themselves dream of success, but it is a process of exploitation that is causing increasing alarm among West Africa-based NGOs such as Save the Children and Caritas...

Mon Emmanuel, one of the first African footballers to play in Europe, claimed that at least 90 per cent of West African players leaving the region are doing so illegally and most will end up on football's growing scrapheap. 'A young footballer can be worth much more than a diamond. It is the parents' fault. They get lulled into this belief that their son can make money in Europe. It obscene wealth and conspicuous consumption as were the 'nobility' before the French Revolution of 1789. In all the major European leagues young men in their twenties are being gifted with unprecedented wealth for playing the game that will mean they never have to do a day's work once they finish. Their tastes tend, to put it mildly,

is a new slave trade. The reality for most young players is further poverty and abuse. In countries like Malaysia, Thailand, Morocco and Tunisia, the players more often than not end up on the street or sleeping 14 to a room. The majority are deported.'

Save the Children's Côte d'Ivoire country manager, Heather Kerr, says that the exploitation of young footballers in the country is a fast-growing concern. 'The links between football and the trafficking of teenagers is deeply concerning. Many parents see in their children "potential geniuses" who will help secure the family's future but they neglect to think about the consequences of turning their children into objects of transaction'...

Sepp Blatter [head of FIFA] said in 2006: 'Europe's leading clubs conduct themselves increasingly as neo-colonialists who don't give a damn about heritage and culture, but engage in social and economic rape.' ◆

Dan McDougall, 'Africa's new slave trade is the price of the beautiful game', *The Observer*, 10 June 2007.

towards the garishly ostentatious. The Manchester United and England right back Gary Neville, for example, may not match his friend David Beckham in terms of looks and charisma, but he has built a vast estate near Bolton including its own cinema, indoor and outdoor swimming pools and a personal golf course. For his wedding in June 2007 he reputedly offered pop singer James Blunt £100,000 ($200,000) to sing 'You're Beautiful' to his bride (but was turned down).

Such easy riches inevitably act as a magnet to talented

boys all over the world. In Africa's shanty towns, in particular, there are thousands of boys dreaming of following the trail blazed by stars such as Chelsea's Didier Drogba and Michael Essien (from Côte d'Ivoire and Ghana respectively). But for every success story there are a thousand failures (see 'New Slave Trade', page 110).

Boys' football in Liberia.

Is there any alternative?

The juggernaut of globalized football seems unstoppable, driven by greed into ever more outlandish territory. Yet within the game itself there is significant anxiety about the path being pursued. It is easy to see why. Globalized market forces have resulted not just in the emergence of five élite European leagues, which are increasingly creaming off the top talent from and impoverishing those in the rest of the world, but of ever-more-dominant top clubs within those leagues.

Increasingly the big clubs are organizing themselves to protect their own interests – primarily aiming to ensure their access to the riches that come with participation in the Champions League. To that end they have formed an organization called G-14, an invitation-only group of the most powerful clubs in Europe (currently 18 strong, despite the name) that acts as a powerful lobbying force. New UEFA President Michel Platini called in 2007 for G14 to disband, describing it as 'élitist'.

The problem is that if the free market in football continues to run riot, football outcomes are bound to become ever more predictable. In smaller nations the problem often reveals itself earlier, as Champions League cash helps ensure that one or two clubs dominate domestic competition year after year, as with Glasgow Celtic and Rangers in Scotland, and Rosenborg in Norway (which has failed to win the Norwegian League only once since 1992). In England, meanwhile, while there were eight different champions in the 1960s there have so far been only three in the 2000s, and in the five years to 2007, only once did a club outside the 'Big Four' qualify for Champions League football. In football at least, economic 'freedom' has a tendency to reduce competition.

PEOPLE'S CLUBS: FC BARCELONA

FC Barcelona is one of the world's great clubs, with a following well beyond its Catalan heartland. It regularly contends against Real Madrid for the Spanish league title and against the continent's other top clubs for the Champions League trophy, which it won as recently as 2006. In 2005-6 it was the second richest club in the world. Yet Barcelona is technically a workers' co-operative, set up as such during the 1930s, when the city was a hotbed of anarchism. During the long, grim years of the Franco dictatorship the Camp Nou stadium remained a focal point both for illicit Catalan nationalism and for leftwing republican protest.

To this day its members, or *socis*, own the club, voting for presidents who present manifestos as to how they will take the club forward. Barcelona is by no means the only example of a football club operating as a mutual organization: in the top tier of Spanish football, Atlético Bilbao, Osasuna and even Real Madrid are also subject to supporters' elections. In Germany both Schalke and Hamburg are also entirely owned by

Salary cap

The irony is that in the perceived ideological home of the free market, the US, professional sport has already wrestled with this kind of problem and emerged with a solution that has reined in the power of the wealthiest teams. A salary cap operates in the top leagues of

 their supporters, while by German rules even those clubs part-owned by private capital must give a majority shareholding to fans. It is no coincidence that ticket prices in Germany are a fraction of those in England. This is the ultimate refutation of the idea that clubs can only be owned and run by supporters at the smallest, most local level.

But popular ownership is not the only thing that sets Barcelona apart. For years the club has held out against the otherwise universal practice of allowing a corporate sponsor to plaster their name all over the players' shirts – which means at the moment, for example, that I have to watch Spurs players running around advertising the supposed virtues of an internet gambling company. Admittedly, Barcelona did receive a premium from Nike, its shirt provider, for the display of its ubiquitous swoosh, but this was still a notable stand, which from the 2006-7 season was somehow made all the more impressive when the club agreed to carry a logo after all, and for no money at all – that of the UN children's organization UNICEF. ◆

American football, basketball and ice hockey, ensuring that it is impossible for any one club to monopolize the most expensive talent. Baseball has so far avoided this route, and a luxury tax penalizing the most expensive payrolls has done little to deter the richest clubs, the New York Yankees and Boston Red Sox, from hoovering up the most attractive free agents. Even in baseball, however, a quasi-socialist 'draft' system applies, whereby the team that finishes last gets priority when it comes to choosing the next generation of college talent. This undoubtedly helps to foster competitiveness, and for the first seven years of the new century no club won the World Series twice. American football's NFL goes even further, with an element of mandatory revenue sharing between the richest and poorest clubs.

Applying US-style sporting principles to European football would not be easy – the 'draft' system, for example, only works in leagues without promotion and relegation. But a salary cap would be possible if it were introduced simultaneously Europewide. Revenue sharing already exists to the extent that the French, German and English leagues negotiate their TV rights collectively, guaranteeing a certain level of payments even to the bottom club. Ensuring that some of the riches accruing from the latest TV deals are fed downward to the lower levels of the game, instead of being swallowed up by ever-more monstrous big clubs, is the very least we should expect.

More than big business

European sports ministers have begun talking about the possibility of reform – the 2006 Independent European Sport Review is to be followed in 2007 by a European Commission White Paper with specific proposals for change. British sports minister Richard Caborn deserved commendation for his doggedness in advancing a different view of the role of sport, and football in particular, that challenged the hegemony of the free market. The review talked of a democratic, European sports model, 'deep-rooted in civil society', in which the biggest professional clubs should have a fundamental connection to sport at the grassroots. It openly contested the recently dominant view of professional sport, especially football, as pure big-business entertainment. Caborn's review pulled some of its punches but did argue that 'competitive balance' needed to be restored by means of salary caps and that UEFA needed to share out Champions League money more fairly.

Even these initial attempts at open discussion have been howled down by the leading clubs (especially those in England) and the first indications are that the White Paper will be pathetically weak, avoiding all the most promising recommendations. There is no indication yet that UEFA or the European Union are anywhere close to the kind of resolution that would be required to bring about meaningful change. Things may well have to get worse – more uncompetitive, more elitist, more predictable

PEOPLE'S RESISTANCE: AFC WIMBLEDON AND FC UNITED

Notable recent examples of popular resistance to the corporate, globalized model of football have come in the shape of two new English football clubs set up by alienated supporters. AFC Wimbledon was established in 2002 by fans of Wimbledon FC who opposed the club's US-style 'franchise' move from its historic home in south London to the new city of Milton Keynes some 100 kilometers away. Run on a semi-professional basis, the club is climbing its way up through the lower leagues and is now in what is effectively the seventh tier of the English game.

A similar breakaway venture was formed in 2005 by Manchester United fans disillusioned by the debt-heavy takeover of their club by US entrepreneurs the Glazer family. FC United

– before they get better. The process of regeneration may not start until football has eaten itself.

The world turns, the ball rolls...

David Beckham takes Victoria, Brooklyn, Romeo and Cruz to California to become the poster boy of Major League Soccer's next big push... In the streets of Kinshasa, capital of the Democratic Republic of Congo, skinny boys play ball with the names of Lomana LuaLua

of Manchester has also enjoyed promotion in its first two seasons and is now in the eighth tier of the national game, though with average attendances higher than at some clubs in the Football League. At both clubs, supporters say they have recovered a sense of community and connection that is increasingly lost in professional football at the highest level.

These are by no means the only positive stories. Supporters' trusts are gaining increasing interest – and beginning to accrue minority shareholdings that at least allow them to attend club meetings. The umbrella movement Supporters Direct, which lobbies for more fan involvement in the game's key organizations, can be reached at www.supporters-direct.org ◆

and Shabani Nonda on their backs. In a country ruined by a kleptomaniac dictator and a decade of civil war, with a national income per person of just $120 a year, they are dreaming of winter nights in the unfashionable English towns of Portsmouth and Blackburn, where for these two Congolese players the streets really are paved with gold... Lionel Messi, Barcelona's Argentinean prodigy, scores a goal for Barcelona in 2007 that is almost a carbon copy of Diego Maradona's famous masterpiece against England in the 1986 World Cup, electrifying pace and mesmeric control taking him from the halfway line past four defenders and then the keeper... Juventus start another Italian season, back at the top level of Serie A after their banishment for match-fixing. With AC Milan as European champions and Italy as World Cup holders, it is as if the Calciopoli scandal never really happened... Following concern that things were running behind schedule, South Africa starts refurbishing ten stadiums in nine cities in preparation for the 2010 World Cup, the first in history to be held in Africa... Chelsea is a year into an eight-year kit sponsorship deal with Adidas, which earns the club £12 million ($24 million) a year. Chief executive Peter Kenyon said when the deal was signed: 'We look forward to working with Adidas, whose vision we share. We believe a global partnership with Adidas will be a huge step in helping the club achieve its long-term strategic goals. Together we can become a formidable team...' A ten-year-old German girl plays keep-up in her backyard – 48, 49, 50 times without the ball hitting the ground. One day, she is sure, she will play for her country, currently the women's world champions... A ten-year-old Pakistani boy begins his sixth hour of work, bending low over his stitching of a ball. One day it will be kicked into a goal on the other side of the world, who knows by whom? One day he will maybe go to school...

CONTACTS & RESOURCES

ORGANIZATIONS

**The Global March
Against Child Labour**
An international movement to
mobilize worldwide efforts to
protect and promote the rights of
all children, especially the right
to receive a free, meaningful
education and to be free from
economic exploitation and from
work likely to be harmful to the
child's development.
www.globalmarch.org/

The Clean Clothes Campaign
An international campaign focused
on improving working conditions in
the global garment and sportswear
industries, and empowering the
workers within them.
www.cleanclothes.org

Supporters Direct
A British group that exists to:
promote and support the concept
of democratic supporter ownership
and representation through
mutual, not-for-profit structures;
promote football clubs as civic and
community institutions; work to
preserve the competitive values
of league football in the United
Kingdom and promote the health
of the game as a whole.
www.supporters-direct.org

READING

David Goldblatt, *The Ball Is
Round: A Global History of Football*
(Viking 2006).

Franklin Foer, *How Football
Explains the World* (Arrow 2005).

Eduardo Galeano, *Football in
Sun and Shadow* (Fourth Estate
1997/2003).

Paul Darby, *Africa, Football and
FIFA: Politics, Colonialism and
Resistance* (Frank Cass 2001).

*Sweet FA? Football Associations,
workers' rights, and the World
Cup*, report by the TUC and Labour
Behind the Label,
www.labourbehindthelabel.org/
content/view/118/52/

*Offside! Labour rights and
sports production in Asia*, Oxfam
Australia report,
www.oxfam.org.au/campaigns/
labour/06report/index.html

TRIGGER ISSUES FROM NEW INTERNATIONALIST

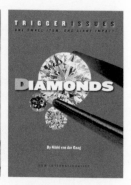

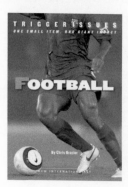